Back To The Basics!

The Three R's: Relevance, Responsibility, and Rewarding Excellence.

by: Kirk Freeman

Dedication:

For the children …. may they feel good about themselves and have teachers and caretakers who allow them to enjoy the educational process!

Acknowledgements:

I want to express my deepest gratitude to my lovely wife and partner, Geri, for her immense patience and love. Her sincere support, unselfish attitude, and sacrifices enabled me to complete this book.

I also want to thank my children, Caleb, Jonah, and Jillian, for understanding when Daddy needed to work in the study to complete his book. Their "unconditional" love was an inspiration.

Lastly, I want to thank my oldest son, Jared, for his support and ideas in writing this book. His leadership, his insights and his helpful hints made this project much easier.

ABOUT THE AUTHOR

Kirk Freeman is a professional consultant who has inspired thousands of educators and parents across the country. He leads workshops and presents keynote speeches on a variety of topics that enable students and teachers alike to "discover excellence!"

Dr. Freeman is a former military officer, classroom teacher, coach, school administrator, and college professor. He has been in the education field for over twenty years. His experiences and expertise allow him to create an environment where "everyone is someone."

Kirk is the founder and president of Kirk Freeman Consulting. He resides in Brazil, Indiana with his wife, Geri, and children, Caleb, Jonah, and Jillian. His oldest son, Jared, is currently a Fourth Class Cadet at the United States Air Force Academy.

Kirk Freeman Consulting

"Discovering Excellence"

The mission is to provide parents and educators with the knowledge, information, and research-based strategies necessary to foster a positive learning environment. Critical thinking, problem solving, and communication skills will be enhanced through this "discovery" process.

Kirk is available for your next conference keynote, staff development workshop, parent workshop, and/or professional consultation.

You may contact Kirk at:

(812) 442-7448 or

kfreeman4004@aol.com

Table of Contents:

Kirk Freeman Consulting
619 West Emerald Drive
Brazil, IN 47834

Cover Design – Geri Freeman and Caleb Freeman

Editor – John Chalos

Book Design – John Chalos

Printed in the United States of America by:
Woodburn Graphics
25 South 6th Street
Terre Haute, IN 47808
1-800-457-0674

Introduction

I have had the privilege of working with a great number of dedicated teachers, students, and parents over the last several years. During the span of my career I've seen many changes take place in our society as well as in the field of education. Americans live in a much different society today than we did ten to twenty years ago. In order to prepare our young people for what they will face in the future, educators must first realize that there has been a shift away from the industrial model of society toward a society based on learning and information.

The word "work" has been redefined in this era. We have to rethink our approach toward traditional training. This rethinking entails focusing more than ever on developing the values, attitudes, and analytical skills which will allow our children to survive and succeed throughout the many career and educational changes they may face in this highly mobile and rapidly changing world. We are in an information/communication age that requires students to have good interpersonal skills and a good sense of the "affective domain" complementing their technical skills.

I have concluded that true learning is a process; not just an end product. Students must grasp the process of learning, rather than simply picking up a fixed skill set, if they are to cope with careers that may change several times during their lifetime.

All too often, school personnel and parents alike get wrapped up in the "Back-to-the Basics" Movement. We begin to tailor our teaching to the old "Three R's: Reading, Riting, and Rithmetic" mantra. Granted, these subjects are important. Yet, I have learned over time that the true "Three R's" should be: Relevance, Responsibility, and Rewarding Excellence. These concepts are the key ingredients needed to ensure that our students develop the proper learning skills necessary to make it possible for them to discover the "excellence" that we all strive to achieve.

A few years ago, I had a student in class whom I will refer to as John Abel. John had been sexually abused by his biological father and had since lived in four foster homes. My encounter with Mr. Abel greatly affected my philosophy on the "Back-to-the-Basics" Movement.

John Abel was on the "six-year" high school plan – he had spent six years trying to earn his diploma. John was taking United States History, attempting to earn the required credit for graduation. He had previously failed the course two times. This time he had me for his teacher. I noticed very quickly that his self-esteem was quite low and that he had a very difficult time making eye contact with anyone.

As an educator, I like to use "active" learning concepts that enable students to discover knowledge and then to apply the information they learn to real-life situations. The classroom was risk-free and positive in nature. Everyone was allowed to make mistakes. John was encouraged to apply his dominant intelligence and work through his preferred learning style to achieve the objectives of the course.

One of the projects that I assigned during the Civil War Unit required each student to prepare a "Civil War bag." Each student was to decorate the outside of a brown paper bag, using it to represent a theme that the student believed symbolized the Civil War. The students were then required to place items into their bag that they believed represented important concepts learned from the war.

Once the bag was prepared, each student would present the contents of his or her bag to the other members of the class. The presenting student would begin the presentation by stating his or her name, after which all other students and myself would applaud.

It was John's turn to present — he waited to present until last. He walked to the front of the room, placed his bag on a table and stood behind the podium. He gripped the podium so tightly that his knuckles turned white. With his head down, and in a whisper, he mumbled, "My name is John Abel."

As the students applauded, John left the podium and exited the room. There was complete silence. After a few seconds (that seemed like an eternity) Mr. Abel returned. He approached the podium once again, looked at the other students and very clearly said, "My name is John Abel!" The other students applauded very loudly.

John, while making eye contact with everyone in the room, presented his "Civil War bag" in an exemplary manner. The presentation was quite a success.

After the class was over John remained seated. After all of the other students exited the classroom, John walked over to me, and with tears in his eyes, said, "Thank you. That is the first time in my entire life that anyone has ever applauded me!"

John Abel's self-concept had changed. He walked with a different "beat" in his step and made eye contact with people. John graduated that year. Currently, he is a productive citizen with a wonderful family.

In my classroom — "PERFECT!" — all students are perfect! John's learning went beyond meeting all of the standards and objectives of the course. He also learned skills relevant to his personal needs while he was in my class. He was held accountable for his own learning. No excuses were made. The choices he made in preparing and presenting the required assignments or "learning tasks" were his own. John was motivated to have his needs met and took advantage of the opportunities to do so. Accomplishing those goals, he felt success and he was rewarded for his learning endeavors. A positive self-concept was cultivated and nurtured. Excellence was rewarded!

The true "Three R's": Relevance, Responsibility, and Rewarding Excellence can be seen in John's example.

This is why I am writing this book. I want other teachers and parents to experience the joys of helping others to grasp the learning process so that they can truly discover excellence for themselves. My journey in education has been rewarding and FUN! I want to help others experience the true Three R's!!

Chapter 1

"Real"ality Check

Making Learning Real — "Real"ality Check

We currently live in an era that considers *standards-based* reform to be the norm. Standardized tests are the bureaucratic measurement system that we use to hold our schools accountable. It is assumed by many of our lawmakers that improved student learning in our schools can only be measured by external test scores. This new accountability system is oversimplified.

Most states have begun giving standardized tests in order to "qualify" their students for graduation. Test scores are being used to decide and judge student performance across the board. As a result of this trend, many schools have employed a policy of "teaching to the test" in order to demonstrate to the state the adequate yearly improvement required of their students.

Does simply teaching kids how to pass state mandated standardized tests ensure that all our students will be able to meet the high standards of learning required for them to become successful in life? Aren't teaching and learning more than just the recalling of facts?

A **"Real"ality Check**, or *making learning real*, is centered on the idea that effective learning involves more than just scoring well on a few tests. (Jones, 2004) When learning is made *real* through effective, quality teaching, students are enabled to process information and complete real world tasks. To obtain a useful understanding of the curriculum that we teach to them, students must be able to research and process information for themselves from numerous sources with complete accuracy.

Dr. Howard Gardner, a leading expert in the field of education and founder of the "Multiple Intelligences" theory, believes that the most productive learning process results when students are actively engaged in projects which are challenging, meaningful, long-term, and complex. (Gardner, 1993) Activities providing complexity, depth, and duration also challenge students to develop the skills needed in order to function effectively in the twenty-first century world – skills such as: initiative, goal-setting, collaboration, planning, the ability to find information and to communicate it to others, the ability to solve problems, and the ability to think critically. (Berliner & Biddle, 1995)

Whenever one completes a **"Real"ality Check,** he or she must pursue the concept of quality learning. I truly believe that quality teaching and *making learning real* are synonymous with quality learning. A teacher should complete regular mental **"Real"ality Checks** on the selected curriculum and the teaching techniques included in his or her repertoire.

Whenever one completes a **"Real"ality Check,** one must consider and pursue opportunites for quality learning. I believe completing a successful **Check** includes the following attributes: *depth, ownership, creativity, and integration.*

The first attribute is **depth.** Instead of using our limited class time to "skim the surface," the teacher should select pertinent and appropriate *objectives* to teach, then allow for the students to discover the vast information pertinent to the topic. Students must be encouraged to analyze and synthesize that information for themselves. One should not attempt to teach a vague overview of everything that pertains to each topic, rather one should limit his or her teaching to the aspects that are indicative of and relate directly to the appropriate state/federal standards for curriculum. Students must be allowed to build good study habits of their own rather than simply benefiting from the teacher's good study habits.

Textbooks are only sources of information; not the curriculum. Therefore, a teacher should not try to cover each and every chapter of the book in order to say that the entire book has been "taught" to the class. Instead, one should select sections from the textbook that assist in learning the objectives of the course of study.

Whenever one goes in-depth, true learning occurs. Not only do the students memorize basic information, they gain the insight needed in order to apply the information they learn to a real-life situation. The students are able to use this information to solve problems.

The second attribute of quality learning that we need to foster in our students is **ownership.** The teacher must allow the students to share in the learning process so that the students can begin to see it as their own responsibility to do what is necessary to make learning real. Our students need to be encouraged to take pride in learning and to establish goals for themselves that demonstrate constant improvement. Students should not be allowed to remain satisfied with the status quo. Instead they must be encouraged to strive for excellence.

The teacher should establish specific goals for the students to reach within definite time-frames while encouraging students to develop their own work ethic and motivational skills. Students need "completion dates" included in their assignments. The brain needs to have concrete deadlines to "shoot for" rather an arbitrary point. Without a due date it becomes harder to focus and there is no closure.

The third attribute of quality learning is **creativity**. Students need to be able to think *out-of-the-box* and develop strategic plans on their own. Critical thinking skills stem from one's ability to use his or her imagination and to work from the higher levels of Bloom's Taxonomy.

One's capacity to develop original thoughts and ideas enables one to "solve problems." In order to effectively function in the twenty-first century, one needs to be able to distinguish which information is most pertinent toward solving a particular problem and then be able to use this information creatively in developing the solution.

Albert Einstein once said that, "Imagination is more important than knowledge… knowledge is limited, but imagination encircles the world. To see with one's own eyes, to feel and judge without succumbing to the suggestive power of the fashion of the day, to be able to express what one has seen and felt in a trim sentence or even in a cunningly wrought word… is that not glorious? When I examine myself and my methods of thought, I come close to the conclusion that the gift of imagination has meant more to me than my talent for absorbing absolute knowledge."

There is no doubt in my mind that a creative thought has the potential to change the world.

Integration is the final attribute of quality learning that I'd like to discuss. Instead of merely being able to show us that they can memorize facts, our students should be able to show us that they can apply the knowledge that they've acquired from their studies. They must be able to use that information away from the classroom in order for it to benefit them. There must be *carry-over* into the *real world.* The knowledge our students acquire must be integrated into their real lives in order for it to be valuable to them.

A student cannot spend a significant amount of time engaging in *in-depth* study without experiencing the integration of the knowledge discovered in that process into his or her activities both inside and outside of the classroom. Constant improvement is seen whenever students learn to find and analyze information for themselves in order to apply it to specific tasks.

Students find learning more fun when they are actively involved in the process – and when they know that their studies can be utilized in real life situations. As in sports, the student needs to be an active participant, not a bench warmer, in order to fully understand the value of the skills he or she has learned in practice or in the classroom.

In order to ensure quality learning – quality teaching

must be utilized. Quality teaching includes presenting appropriate challenges for each individual student and outlining appropriate expectations. Students need to know what their objectives are – *it's nearly impossible to hit a moving target!* – but they also need to reach that objective on their own steam. The role of the teacher must change from being the *sage on the stage* to the *guide on the side.* The teacher must become a facilitator.

Quality teachers also need to learn to create a risk-free environment that cultivates confidence in their students. Whenever the environment is conducive to learning, students know it is okay to take risks and move out of their comfort zones. Students need to know that it is okay to fail or they won't feel comfortable taking chances. In fact, the teacher should hope that students make mistakes in class. Those mistakes are golden opportunities for a quality learning experience.

A quality teacher also needs to have a love and a passion for learning, as well as for teaching. Quality teachers need to model good learning in their own behavior if they are to expect their students to value it.

Appropriate resources need to be available in order for students to discover knowledge. Students must then be taught how to ask the appropriate questions in order to get the information they need from those resources to develop the solutions to their problems.

Problem solving situations must be presented to the students. Teachers MUST create the opportunities for success!

Deduction and *"Experiencial Learning"*

I contend that there are two thought processes that are used in education — *deductive learning* and *"experiencial learning."*

Deductive learning is a process in which a conclusion is drawn from specific information given to the student by the teacher. The information given is usually designed to lead the student to a specific conclusion. The conclusions being made are generated by the teacher's outline and from the teacher's perspective; not the student's. This process is definitely teacher driven.

The overwhelming majority of classroom time is spent in this mode of "teaching." Students are not given the opportunity to apply information from their own studies or experiences, but rather they are channeled in a direction and encouraged to draw conclusions exclusively from the information given to them by the teacher.

Unfortunately, much of this information drains right through the student's brain. The brain is like a sieve; not a sponge. It latches onto what it can relate to and lets the rest drain right on through.

A meaningful comparison between the information presented to them and their own point of view must be fostered before students can learn. If this is not done, it can sometimes lead to what I call "chop-logic."

"Chop-logic" is what occurs whenever students make inferences that are drawn from the teacher's perspective, which has been presented to them in class, rather than integrating their own experiences into the discussion. Sometimes, the objectives are confused by the student because he or she can't identify with the information. The result is "chop-logic." An example of "chop-logic" is as follows:

Proof that Kirk is a good golfer!

1. Kirk is a male.
2. Male is a homonym of mail.
3. Mail is delivered by the postal service.
4. The postal service uses airplanes.
5. Airplanes are flown at the United States Air Force Academy.
6. The United States Air Force Academy's mascot is the falcon.
7. The falcon is a relative to the eagle.
8. An eagle is scored by a good golfer.

Therefore, Kirk is a good golfer!

The other thought process used in education is *"experiencial learning."* Though it is not used much in school today, the majority of true learning occurs from this process. **"Experiencial learning"** is the process of arriving at a generalization based on personal experiences.

Students draw from their own experiences whenever a teacher is using this teaching method. Students are able to relate the *learning situation* to their *real life situations.* Students are able to make an emotional connection to the new information based on their own relevant experiences. A student's brain is able to integrate this new information and retrieve it when necessary because he or she considers it relevant.

Enhanced learning takes place whenever one is involved in this type of learning process. *"Experiencial learning"* promotes much more student involvement in the process. Every teacher's goal should be to move from lecturing to methods of teaching that require more active student participation, such as: presenting, cooperative learning, mentoring, simulations, and live events.

Based on my professional experiences, I have ranked the methods utilized by classroom teachers from *low retention rate* to *high retention rate* as follows:

Retention Rate Scale

Method:	Retention Rate:
Lecture	Low
Reading	
Demonstrations	
Cooperative Learning	Medium
Simulations	
Real-Life Learning	
Teaching/Coaching	High

The ultimate **"Real"ality Check** ensures that learning is purposeful. Worthwhile learning enables people to utilize prior knowledge in the understanding of new information. The brain *chunks* new information into storage on information that was previously obtained. Patterns develop in order for new knowledge to be placed in long-term memory.

Purposeful learning also requires a sense of relevance and emotion. An emotional involvement in the learning process excites the individual and triggers the storage of the information being taught.

The brain is an amazing organ. It is bombarded with thousands of stimuli each day yet it selects the input that has **relevance** and allows other information to dissolve and fade away.

Our emotions assist in determining the relevance of that data. Take a moment to recall your first learning experience. Yes, it is normally something that had emotion involved with it. The person assisting you with the process was usually a nurturing individual whom you trusted. There was an emotional connection.

Geoffrey Caine, a leading expert on the brain, says that we are driven to search for meaning. Because we have a social brain, it is important to build authentic relationships in the classroom and at home. True learning is enhanced by challenge and inhibited by threat.

Thinking and *feeling* are connected, because our learning *patterns are* based on our emotions. If we hope to make an impact, we need to help students create a sense of **relationship** with the subject matter in addition to enhancing their intellectual understanding of it. (D'Arcangelo, Diamond, Wolfe, Sylwester, Caine, & Caine, 2004)

Utilizing *brain-based* learning concepts and utilizing a **"Real"ality Check** enables teachers to make the subjects they are teaching more applicable for the students.

Developing a more *differentiated* set of effective teaching techniques will allow teachers to tailor their instruction to the needs of their individual students. Including all of the ideas presented in this chapter will enable teachers to create an environment in which **ALL** students can **LEARN.**

The *"Real"ality checkup* will be a positive one.

Listed below are Doc's helpful hints relating to making learning real. The hints are suggestions to improve teaching and to assist in the learning process.

DOC'S HELPFUL HINTS:

Use differentiated instruction.

Differentiated instruction is a method of instruction that utilizes multiple teaching techniques so that students in the class with different abilities and learning needs can experience the appropriate amount of individualization. This involves finding many ways to use, develop, and present concepts as part of the learning process.

Differentiated instruction is proactive. It provides multiple approaches to delivering the content, process, and product of the curriculum. It is definitely *student-centered.* When utilizing differentiated learning, engage all of the students and emphasize the development of creative and critical thinking skills.

When implementing differentiated instruction, there will be a balance between *student-selected* and *teacher-assigned* tasks and working arrangements. There should be a pervasive expectation of growth in the classroom – students and teachers collaborating together to achieve learning and success. We need to teach children to think for themselves and to become problem solvers.

Incorporate cooperative learning.

Interpersonal skills are needed for children to survive in the twenty-first century. These skills should be taught along with the subject matter content. Students need to understand that interpersonal skills are intertwined with good communication and problem solving skills.

Teachers do the majority of the talking in a typical classroom. On average, children only talk one-and-one-half minutes per day on task. It is amazing that school systems will spend such an inordinate amount of money transporting children to a central location (a school building) only to make them sit silently in a classroom rather than participate in their own learning. Teachers are doing the work and students are being forced to be *passive learners.* Learning should not be a spectator sport. Students should be active participants in the learning process.

Cooperative learning is the most researched teaching strategy of all time. Benefits of cooperative learning include:

Higher achievement

Increased retention

Greater use of higher level reasoning

Greater intrinsic motivation

More positive heterogeneous relationships

Better attitudes toward school

Better attitudes toward teachers

Higher self-esteem

Greater social support

More positive psychological adjustment

More on-task behavior

Greater collaborative skills

Use the "experiencial" thought process.

Students need to learn with their hearts. Content becomes meaningful whenever students use their own experiences as part of the learning process. Learning from our hearts involves our emotions. Our emotions enable the brain to develop memory pathways and connections.

Teachers and parents should create opportunities for children to integrate knowledge into their daily lives. Individualizing the instruction allows children to draw upon their own background when applying the information. Allow children to relate the learning situation to *real life* scenarios.

Remember the "Less is More" concept.

I hate to admit this, but when I started teaching, I thought that my textbook was my curriculum. When teaching United States History, I would begin with chapter one and proceed chapter by chapter in numerical sequence. At the end of the school year, I would cram the last several chapters into a three week period. *I covered the material!* But, not much learning took place. (I need to send my former students an apology letter!)

Knowing what I know today, I recommend that teachers develop a curriculum centered on the required state standards. Instead of "teaching the textbook," use the book as a tool. Spend ample time on each standard. Utilize the textbook, the Internet, other reference guides, et al., to assist with the lesson. One can even use sections based out of multiple chapters to teach a specific standard.

By covering less material in a more in-depth manner, you are encouraging students to "dig deeper" instead of just "scratching the surface" when they study. Whenever the higher levels of Bloom's Taxonomy are used, students receive a bonus as a result – the recall of factual information is enhanced. In other words, students exercise the lower levels of thinking (knowledge and comprehension) whenever they utilize the higher level thinking skills such as application, analysis, synthesis, and evaluation.

Instill a sense of "ownership."

Jill was walking down the hallway with a spring in her step and a smile on her face. As we got closer to one another, I heard her say, "I love that class!" I stopped and commented to her that it appeared that she was having a "perfect" day. Jill informed me that she was really enjoying the way Ms. Stewart was teaching her English class.

I questioned her about what made this such a great class. Jill went on to say, "Instead of diagramming sentences and completing worksheets, Ms. Stewart asked us to write a short story that we will be sharing with local elementary school students. Once we write the initial draft of the story, we will be placed in cooperative groups to complete peer reviews. We will assist one another with the grammatical part of writing along with the creative issues."

After catching her breath, Jill continued, "The next step will be to rewrite the short story. Once the story is completed, we will read it to grade school children who are just learning to read. How exciting and practical this assignment is!"

This excitement is present whenever students take ownership in their own learning. Instead of just going through the motions, Jill was allowed to select her own topic and learn the English standards based on this *real-world* project. There is relevance in Jill's English class. She has taken ownership in learning all aspects of the writing process. Ms. Stewart does not have to prepare numerous worksheets to get the objective met. Jill has accepted her major role in the PROCESS!

Allow children to be critical thinkers and problem solvers.

Critical thinking is the process we use to analyze and develop ideas. It is a process that allows us to:

> Make inferences.
> Compare and contrast ideas.
> Categorize and sequence options.
> Make effective decisions.

In today's world, children need to be able to use these critical thinking skills to survive. The work force has become one that requires problem solving capabilities.

Today, life is very complex. We are required to make several decisions in a day's time. Many of these decisions relate to complex issues. It is an exciting time, but one that demands that we think on our feet and use higher level thinking skills in our decision making process.

Problem solving has become a norm in our culture. We solve problems in our personal relationships, at school, at work, and in our homes. Allow children to be creative, thus enabling them to develop a way of expressing meaningful, new connections.

Students should be given the opportunity to develop creative problem solving techniques. Creative thinking is a process that allows us to:

> Recognize challenges, concerns, and opportunities.
> Think of new and unusual possibilities.
> Think and experience different viewpoints.
> Elaborate and extend alternatives.

When one utilizes Doc's helpful hints, students are able to DISCOVER excellence through the use of a PERFECT process!

Chapter 2

Brain-Based Learning

Brain-Based Learning

Brain research is normally not directed at making improvements in traditional learning processes, but several of the more recent studies have opened up new avenues toward improving teaching techniques. Understanding how and when the brain learns best will assist us in ensuring that all students learn.

Using the latest research to validate our teaching practices brings more credibility to the teaching profession. There has been more brain research conducted in the last ten years than in all previous years combined. WOW! What opportunities we have to make a difference in each child's life!

The following areas will be addressed in this chapter:

> Brain Facts
>
> Windows of Opportunity
>
> Enriched Environment
>
> Emotions
>
> Gender Differences

Brain Facts:

Our brains are amazing organs comprised of 100 billion nerve cells called neurons. The brain consists of four lobes. It weighs approximately three pounds accounting for only two percent of an individual's total body weight. Seventy-eight percent of the brain is made up of water. It uses twenty percent of the body's energy. The brain's most distinguishing features are its many folds. These wrinkles are part of the cerebral cortex. The cerebral cortex is folded over upon itself. If unfolded, it would be the size of a pillowcase.

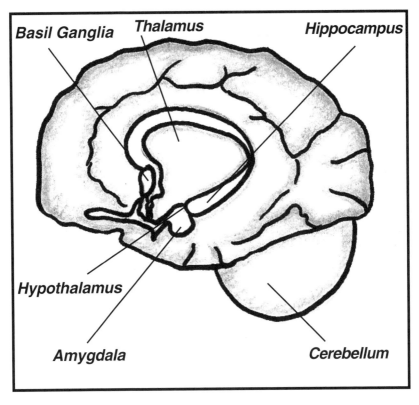

Thalamus: *The sorting station for sensory input.*

Hypothalamus: *The brain's thermostat, regulating bodily functions.*

Basil Ganglia: *The area responsible for motor function.*

Amygdala: *Processes intense emotions.*

Hippocampus: *Responsible for the formation of explicit long-term memories.*

Cerebellum: *Involved in posture, coordination, balance, motor memory, novelty learning, and other cognitive activities. (Jensen, 1998)*

The brain has two hemispheres — the left and right cerebrum. Approximately 250 million nerves form a bundle connecting the two hemispheres. This area is known as the Corpus Callosum. In general, the left side processes "parts" and the right side processes "wholes." Both cerebrum are important to learning. (Jensen, 1995)

The left hemisphere processes information sequentially. Almost one-half of left-handers use their right hemisphere for language. Fine motor skills are normally a left hemisphere activity while gross motor functions are controlled by the right side of the brain. The right hemisphere recognizes negative emotions at a faster pace while the left hemisphere detects positive feelings faster. Sometimes the hemispheres we utilize for different functions change over time. (Jensen, 1998)

The brain is comprised of four lobes. The lobe located in the middle portion of the back of the brain, called the occipital lobe, is primarily responsible for vision.

Judgment, creativity, problem solving, and planning are handled in the area around the forehead called the frontal lobe.

The parietal lobe is responsible for language. It is located on the top of the back area of the brain.

On the left and right sides of the brain we find the temporal lobes which are primarily responsible for hearing, memory, meaning, and language.

There are overlaps in the various functions of the four lobes. (Jensen, 1998)

Having learned how the human brain operates best, scientists now believe that learning is a three step process.

First, the introduction of a *stimulus* to the brain starts the process. This stimulus can be something new or something we already know. If it is a repeat of earlier learning, the probability is that the neural pathways will become more efficient. As long as the new information is coherent, this "stimulation" produces greater beneficial electrical energy than the "old" information.

The second step in the learning process is the *sorting and processing* of the stimulus. Once the stimulus is received, the brain cells act as tiny electrical batteries. Changes in voltage assist in transmitting signals for dendrite growth. Dendrites are extensions (strand-like fibers) emanating from the neuron. The repeated electrical stimulation fosters all growth by the way of dendrite branching.

Lastly, there is a formation of *memory potential.* The dendrites branch out and assist us in making more connections which ultimately help us understand better. The pieces are in place so that memory can be easily activated.

An important point to take note of is that we do not have "memory banks." Instead, we have "pathways" for specific types of learning. Our brain does not store memories, but instead it recreates them.

Retrieval is better when the learning situation is "real." Rote learning creates difficulties for most students since there is not relevance in the process. (Jensen, 1998)

Windows of Opportunity:

Windows of opportunity are critical periods during which the brain is at its peak for learning in a specific area. (Fogarty, 1997) Human beings experience a great deal of growth in dendrite formation during their first eight to ten years. After that time period, the branches that have not made connections die off. The cortex grows rapidly, reaches a peak, and then slowly decreases. If we are placed in an enriched environment whenever the cortex begins to slow down, it will begin to grow again. Therefore, we should continue stimulating our children in the learning process by providing an enriched environment for them.

Robert Sylwester, Professor Emeritus of Education at the University of Oregon at Eugene, points out that the ideal time to master a skill associated with a system is just when a new system is coming on line in your brain.

Language is a good example of this. It is easy for a two-or-three year-old to learn any language. If one waits to learn a new language later in life, it is much more difficult because the systems governing this type of learning are being used for something else.

In short, we do have optimal learning times, but the brain's capacity for learning and change is limitless, depending on our willingness to seek new experiences and opportunities. (D'Arcangelo, Diamond, Wolfe, Sylwester,Caine, & Caine, 2004)

As mentioned, we have optimal times in which it is easier to develop certain concepts. Once these windows are passed, the learning process is changed. Some of these windows of opportunity include:

Birth to three years old: We learn the foundations for language development, muscle control, emotional development, and intellectual development.

One year to ten years old: We learn emotional phrasing and generic vocabulary.

1. Ideal time to learn a foreign language.
2. Ideal time to learn how to play musical instruments and appreciate music.

Three to ten years old: We learn math and logic vocabulary.

Ten plus years old: The best time to develop complex math/logic patterns and development of grammar and spelling.

It is believed that if these "opportunities" are missed, the child may develop the skill later in life but not at the same proficiency and/or ease. When children learn certain skills later in life they utilize different segments of the brain to accomplish that learning than they would have if they had learned those skills in the natural course of events at the proper time. (Healy, 1990)

Enriched Environment:

An enriched environment is critical in assisting the learner. The environment should be one in which the learning process is challenging, yet risk-free.

New information and experiences should be presented and students should be allowed to interact with this new stimuli through the use of *"experiencial thinking"* — the process of learning new information by relating it to one's own experiences. As I said before, most learning is done *"experiencially."*

Students should be given the opportunity to draw upon their past experiences. Fear should be nonexistent in the classroom. The quickest way to "shut down" the brain is to allow fear and anxiety to keep your students from stepping out and taking risks. The environment in our classrooms must be risk-free — students must feel free to make mistakes. Trial and error are important aspects of the discovery process.

Challenging your students at the proper level of difficulty is important. If you make your challenges too difficult or too easy then students will either give up or get bored. Mental challenges should include the presenting of new information with varying degrees of difficulty, variation in the time required to complete tasks and projects, and variation in the amount of support given by the instructor. Variation is important. Novelty is important. Change the look of the classroom and the instructional strategies. Include teaching that takes advantage of all nine of the *intelligences* (see chapter three) and uses authentic methods of assessment. (Jensen, 1998)

Another key component necessary for an enriched environment is positive feedback. The brain is designed to operate based on the feedback it receives. (Harth, 1995) Without feedback, we are unable to learn.

Several conditions are required to make the feedback we give our students effective. The feedback given should be specific, immediate, and it should reflect the results of the choices made by the student. (Jensen, 1998)

An enriched environment is a *brain-friendly* place. An enriched classroom is safe and has a balance of direct instruction for skill development and authentic learning tools that allow the students to experience challenging situations. Techniques which meet the unique needs of each learner and foster opportunities for each one to utilize *"experiencial learning"* and integrate the new information learned into his or her real-life situation should be present in every classroom. (Fogarty, 1997)

Marian Diamond, a neuroscientist and professor of neuroanatomy at the University of California at Berkeley, has conducted research that documents the influence of the environment on the growth of brain cells.

Dr. Diamond completed a study working with rats that investigated the changes in the structure of the nerve cells in the cerebral cortex when rats were exposed to either an impoverished or enriched environment. Rats living in an enriched environment grew more dendrites which developed a thicker cortex. Dendrites are the major receptive surface of the nerve cell. By interacting with other rats and with objects to climb on and explore, their cortex had grown.

In contrast, the rats that sat and watched the other rats had fewer measurable changes than the rats that were actually allowed to participate. The enriched environment allowed dendrite growth which changes the structure and chemistry of the brain which is called "plasticity."

We are all different; therefore, teachers and parents need to provide an environment in which all children can think for themselves and be "actively" engaged in the learning process. We need to encourage all of our students, not just the most outgoing of the bunch, to talk to one another and to ask questions in class. Students need to be allowed to work in groups and they need to be allowed to participate in their own learning process. (D'Arcangelo, Diamond, Wolfe, Sylwester, Caine, & Caine, 2004)

In short, an enriched classroom creates opportunities for students to discover knowledge and apply the new concepts learned to new situations in a risk-free environment.

Emotions:

Emotions affect our health, our survival instincts, our memory, and our learning. Positive emotions can foster a love for learning. They can increase our motivation to learn and build our self-confidence. On the other hand, negative emotions can detrimentally affect one's desire to learn. (Jensen, 1998) Our feelings and emotions affect our capacity to learn by stimulating and activating our brain.

What we remember most from our childhood deals with our emotional times — either our lowest "lows" or our highest "highs." We need to keep that in mind when educating young people and remember to engage our students' emotions in the learning process and make their learning personally compelling. (Jensen, 1995)

Anything that involves our emotions gets our attention. Our emotional system drives our *attention system*, which in turn guides our ability to learn and memorize things. It is biologically impossible to learn and remember anything when we are not paying attention. Whether we consider something important or not is determined by our emotional system. If we do not engage their emotions in the learning process, students will not value our efforts to educate them and they will begin to feel a void that they will seek to fill elsewhere — and it may not be in school or at home. (D'Arcangelo, Diamond, Wolfe, Sylwester, Caine, & Caine, 2004)

When we feel stressed, our bodies go through a chemical reaction. Our adrenal glands release a peptide called cortisol. This triggers numerous physical reactions including increased blood pressure, tensing of the large muscles, and depression of the immune system.

Chronic stress can lead to more absenteeism, impair a student's ability to sort out what is important and what is not important, and inhibit his or her ability to form long-term memories. (Jacobs & Nadel, 1985)

A stressful environment is linked to failure. Students learning in a low stress environment are free to develop relationships, take risks and integrate a wider range of materials and experiences into their education. Stress and the threat of humiliation must be taken out of the learning environment in order to achieve the maximum results. (Jensen, 1998)

According to Eric Jensen, some of the key steps that assist us in promoting a stress-free learning environment are as follows. Making learning purposeful for the students by engaging their positive emotions and by showing your own enthusiasm. Employing interactive group activities such as drama, role-playing, large-scale projects, and celebrations. Putting students into a good emotional state prior to presenting the information to them. Including opportunities for students to express their emotions after a learning experience. (Jenson 1995)

Gender Differences:

In order to ensure that all of our students are given the best education possible it is important for educators to understand that there are definite gender differences. By learning about and understanding these differences, we can modify and develop appropriate teaching strategies that will assist both the male and the female students on a more personal level.

The following chart points out some of the differences that exist between our male and female students based on the statistical averages.

Males:	Females:
Males experience an earlier specialization of the right brain; this causes a tendency to experience more difficulty learning linguistic skills.	Females experience an early specialization of verbal skills; often read better.
Males have more difficulty discussing their emotions.	Females find it easier to discuss their emotions.
Males express themselves by using gestures and by giving gifts.	Females tend to express themselves verbally.
Males prefer using geometry (maps) when finding places.	Females prefer using landmarks (memory) for finding places.

The male brain is 15% larger at birth, but males lose brain tissue at three times the rate of females.

Hormonal levels are the greatest indicators of gender-related differences in the areas of problem solving and thinking. In the male, the testosterone levels correlate with aggression, competition, and self-confidence. In the female, when estrogen and progesterone levels are high, math and spatial abilities tend to be lower. (Fogarty, 1997)

There are definite differences in how the male and female brains develop. Boys show an earlier specialization of the right brain than girls do. This means that a girl's brain has a longer span of plasticity than that of a boy's; therefore, her brain stays open to growth for more years than the boy's brain. Meanwhile, boys are much more physical than girls at an early age because that part of the brain has developed earlier.

There are also differences in how males and females process input. (Jensen, 1995) A summary of some of the differences:

Hearing: The female is better able to recognize and depict music, nuances of voice, and other sounds.

Touch: Females are more sensitive to touch. They are also superior in performing new motor combinations.

Activity: Male infants play more with objects, much more often than do girls. Females are more responsive to their friends.

Listed below are Doc's helpful hints relating to Brain-Based learning. The hints are suggestions to improve teaching and to assist in the learning process.

DOC'S HELPFUL HINTS:

Now that we've developed a basic understanding of the brain, specific strategies and suggestions need to be addressed to ensure that we can assist our students in obtaining higher academic achievement. This section of the chapter will present suggestions to improve teaching and ultimately improve student learning:

Maintain high expectations.

Using Brain-Based learning strategies enhances the learning process. When individualized, instruction becomes more personal and valuable to the child, therefore more of the instruction is retained and learned. Set your expectations high, tailor your instruction to each unique student, and allow the child to accomplish academic excellence. Do not settle for mediocrity.

Have students establish positive short-term and long-term goals.

Give students time to reflect upon and develop their personal goals. Have them establish goals to be accomplished at the end of a grading period, goals to be accomplished at the end of the semester, along with goals to be accomplished by the end of the school year and beyond.

Alternate between the "big picture" and the "details."

Have you ever tried to put together a jigsaw puzzle without knowing what the end product should look like? This is very difficult because the brain wants to know the "big picture." The same is true in learning. Teachers should give students the opportunity to understand the importance of the entire process. Children, after seeing the "big picture" also need time to work on the details. Demonstrating the relationship between the "whole" and the "pieces" creates an optimal atmosphere for learning.

Encourage students to get plenty of rest but also pursue plenty of activity in their daily lives.

We are becoming a "couch potato" society. Instead of spending hours upon hours watching television and/or playing "sit-down" games, encourage the children in your care to go outside and **PLAY.** Children need plenty of exercise and play in order to help stimulate the brain.

I recommend that children receive plenty of sleep. An elementary age child should receive at least ten to twelve hours of sleep per night. High school students should be receiving at least eight to ten hours of sleep per night. The brain needs this *downtime* in order to process the day's information.

Be sure the learner drinks plenty of water.

Water in the body is needed for the brain to be at its peak performance. We should drink between eight to ten glasses of water per day. I recommend that students, in the elementary grades, keep a water bottle at their desks and continuously drink water throughout the school day.

"Pre-expose" the learner to the topic before officially starting it.

Teachers should introduce students to the background of a new topic prior to beginning that unit of study. This background information enables students to relate to the topic better and draw more *meaning* from the information. This *pre-exposure* to the topic assists children in making an emotional connection and learning from the heart.

Let students know why they are learning the information.

Give them a "Compelling Why." Present a compelling motivation for learning to the students before each lesson. Let children know that there is a purpose to the lesson and that the information learned will benefit them. Whenever a child asks, "Why do I need to learn this?" please do not respond with, "Because I said so!!"

Use all levels of Bloom's Taxonomy.

The overwhelming majority of classroom instruction never allows children to get beyond the two lowest levels of Bloom's Taxonomy — *knowledge and comprehension.* In order to develop as critical thinkers and effective problem solvers, students must be encouraged to develop the higher order thought processes discussed in Bloom's Taxonomy — *application, analysis, synthesis, and evaluation.*

Use creative activities as part of the learning process.

Creative thinking is a vital element in the learning process. In order to produce lateral thinkers, teachers need to encourage students to use creative problem solving strategies. There is no positive correlation between I.Q. and creativity; therefore, **ALL** students can be creative. Give them the opportunity to be *"out-of-box"* thinkers.

Provide opportunities for learners to stop and discuss the material.

Our brains need *downtime* to process information. Teachers, after completing a learning activity, need to give children time (a couple of minutes) to stop and do nothing for a moment. The brain is doing something very important during this time — it is developing and strengthening new, neural pathways.

Introduce short modules of learning.

Educators need to break the instruction time down into small increments. After seven-to-ten minutes, students need a change of pace. A quick celebration, allowing students to get up and move around, will provide the needed break.

After ten minutes of concentration (fifteen at the most) young learners begin to lose focus. The physical movement and "change-of-state" enables the brain to draw "closure" on the information and get prepared for the new information to follow.

Incorporate the different learning styles.

We all learn differently. Why make learning difficult for children? We need to both "teach" and "facilitate" in the style that each learner relishes in order to make the learning process valuable to the students.

The *learning styles* are: kinesthetic, tactual, visual, and auditory. We need to allow children to learn in the style they find most easy and encourage them to enjoy the process.

Include all nine intelligences in your teaching repertoire.

All children are smart! Instead of labeling a child based on their I.Q. score, teachers should seek to find out how the child is smart. Chapter three of this book is devoted to this topic.

Use energizers that require students to move around.

We remember things by developing emotional patterns. These emotional patterns center on location and/or episodes (this is called episodic memory).

After you complete a particular learning segment, allow students to get up and move to a new location before beginning the next learning segment. The brain is developing a learning pattern based on the new location.

Use cross-laterals — arm and leg crossover activities.

Moving the arms and/or legs across the midsection of our bodies is called a cross-lateral motion. The crossover of arms and/or legs assists both brain hemispheres to "talk" to each other. This physical movement assists information to go between the right and left hemispheres of the brain.

Utilize patterns in the learning process.

Knowing that memory requires emotional patterns to be developed, we can assist the process by developing patterns with our students. A wonderful activity to facilitate this is the "beanbag" toss.

1. Place ten to fifteen students in a circle.

2. A child will state to the other participants something that he or she found relevant from the previous learning activity and then toss the beanbag to someone across the circle.

3. The person receiving the beanbag will say what he or she found relevant and then toss the bag to someone else in the circle.

4. The process continues until everyone in the circle has taken a turn.

5. Have the group perform three rounds maintaining the pattern (each person throws the beanbag to the same person he or she threw it to the first time).

6. After three rounds, play a game maintaining the same pattern. Either have the students determine how fast they can get the beanbag moving or determine how many beanbags they can keep moving at the same time.

Ask thought-provoking, open-ended questions.

Children need to develop the ability to respond to open-ended questions. A closed-ended question only requires a "yes" or "no" response. Usually, students will respond to such a question without using higher order thinking skills. Open-ended questions give students the opportunity to use all of the processes in Bloom's Taxonomy. These questions enhance critical thinking and problem solving skills.

Give positive feedback.

Success breeds success! Teachers and parents need to give immediate, positive feedback and give it often. Giving positive feedback allows children to know how well they performed and how they must perform in order to improve the task in the future. Remember that criticism creates cynicism. Negative feedback is not as effective as a positive, feed-forward statement. Be sure to make your suggestions without tearing down the child's self-esteem.

Create a safe learning environment.

Before a child can be convinced to step out and try new things, he or she must feel that the learning environment is risk-free. Children need to know and believe that the learning environment is physically, emotionally, and mentally safe for them. Students need to be able to take risks, knowing that it is okay to fail. It is the **PROCESS** that is important. Establish *esprit-de-corps* in the classroom. Fear and boredom are the quickest ways to "shut down" the brain. They must be eliminated in our classrooms.

Add variety to the environment.

Variety is the spice of life. Include music, games, simulations, props, skits, field trips, guest speakers, etc. in the learning process. Even though some routine is good, students need a "change-of-pace" to remain interested and attentive. Make learning real and **FUN!** Do the unordinary; the unexpected!!

When one utilizes Doc's helpful hints, students are able to DISCOVER excellence through the use of a PERFECT process!

My intent in this chapter has been to give you some "user-friendly" information that will assist in making learning easier, relevant, and pertinent for your students. I am concluding this chapter with a list of fifty ways to discover excellence using Brain-Based strategies.

"50 Ways to Discover Excellence... the Brain-Based Way!"

Model the joy of teaching/ learning

Have positive attitude

Use good listening skills

Use cross-laterals

Make contact with the students

Make connections

Use open-ended questions

Teach skills for life

Use cooperative learning

Have FUN!

Use celebrations

Utilize appropriate practice

Encourage risk-taking

Use guest speakers

Use simulations

Utilize live-event learning

Praise student's accomplishments

Develop intrinsic/extrinsic rewards

Develop lateral thinking

Develop possibility thinking

Give reflection time

Incorporate metacognition

Give feedforward statements

Utilize active learning

Develop critical thinking skills

Create problem solvers

Allow/encourage mistakes

Create an enriched environment

Use music

Be a motivator

Encourage arguments

Utilize the multiple intelligences

Incorporate learning styles

Incorporate sensory (temperament) styles

Use authentic assessments

Make learning relevant

Use compelling why's

Develop safe environment

Do not tolerate "put-downs"

Give choices

Collaborate

Use energizers

Have a passion for learning

Set positive goals

Differentiate learning

Assign reasonable tasks

Share the power

Use mentoring/coaching

Like what you do

Make contact with homes

Chapter 3

Multiple Intelligences

Multiple Intelligences

"Wow! Did you see how John dissected it, studied each of the parts, evaluated what was causing the energy problem, and fashioned it back together so that it was running better than ever?" This sounds like a description of a heart specialist. It could be. Or it could be describing a mechanic... or a heating and cooling specialist... or....

Smart!! Yes, all children are smart!! We need to determine how the children are smart; not whether or not they are smart.

Most people are living under the assumption that there is a level of intelligence and that it is determined by administering standardized tests and thereby computing an intelligence quotient (I.Q.). Once this number is determined, each person is labeled for life. One's "smartness" is determined by what score he or she earned in a setting that most people would never choose. There is a problem with measuring potential in that fashion.

In 1904, Alfred Binet developed this scale in order to identify those students who would most benefit from special services. Binet did not intend for this measuring tool to be used to rank students or to identify their innate potential. (Binet & Simon, 1905)

In 1983, Dr. Howard Gardner, a Harvard Professor, wrote Frames of Mind, a book which revolutionized education. The theory of "multiple intelligences" has impacted the learning process and given parents and teachers much needed information pertaining to the notion that there is more than one type of intelligence.

Gardner studied savants, autistics, and children with learning disabilities, then synthesized the results of his research to develop the theory of multiple intelligences. He did not believe that intelligence could be considered a single quality nor that it could be measured by a single number.

Dr. Gardner's definition of intelligence is more complex than Binet's. He takes into consideration one's ability to solve a problem or one's ability to fashion a product which is valued by the contemporary culture in which one lives. He measures different types of intelligence by differing standards. (Gardner, 1993)

Mindy Lirnhaber, Mara Krechevsky, and Howard Gardner argue that the definitions of intelligences are determined by the location, time, and culture in which they evolve. (Dornhaber et al., 1990)

Logical-mathematical intelligence and linguistic intelligence are generally esteemed in Western culture. Thus, we place tremendous emphasis on language arts and mathematics in our schools today. Both of these intelligences are extremely important, but so are the other intelligences that humans possess. Many people believe the overemphasis of our educational system upon language arts and logical skills has shortchanged those students whose talents lie in other forms of intelligence. (Armstrong, 1994; Gardner, 1993; Haggerty, 1995; Lazear, 1991)

Traditional assessment devices for measuring an individual student's potential or achievement have focused almost exclusively upon the language and math domains. (Gardner, 1993) One of the obvious limitations of such traditional tests of intelligence is that they utilize tasks that do not have authentic counterparts in the world outside of the educational arena. (Karnhaber, et al., 1990)

Dr. Gardner's theory serves as an avenue to develop effective and affective teaching/learning strategies for the classroom.

Dr. Gardner divides the fields of intelligence into the

following categories:

The intelligences include:

Logical-Mathematical: *the intelligence of reasoning and numbers (Number Smart)*

Verbal-Linguistic: *the intelligence of words (Word Smart)*

Visual-Spatial: *the intelligence of images and pictures (Picture Smart)*

Musical-Rhythmic: *the intelligence of tone, rhythm, and timbre (Music Smart)*

Interpersonal: *the intelligence of social understanding (People Smart)*

Intrapersonal: *the intelligence of self-knowledge (Self Smart)*

Bodily-Kinesthetic: *the intelligence of whole body and hands (Body/Movement Smart)*

Naturalist: *the intelligence of recognizing/classifying plants and diagramming relationships (Nature Smart)*

Existential: *the intelligence of understanding one's existence (Big Picture Smart)*

* Existential is just being recognized as the ninth intelligence as this book is being written.

Dr. Gardner (1993) suggests instruction should focus upon providing students with opportunities to discover their specialized interests and unique talents. Everyone should be allowed to develop the talents they possess.

When this type of free exploration is allowed to take place in our learning environments it results in what is called "crystallizing experiences" – the strong emotional attraction to a specific discipline, area, and/or skill. (Krechevsky & Gardner, 1990)

Thomas Armstrong contends that the reverse is true as well. Significant negative encounters tend to "paralyze" or "shut down" specific types of intelligence. Teachers should be careful not to inhibit children from developing their specific skills and talents.

The kinds of skills and knowledge needed for critical thinking and problem solving in one domain of intelligence are independent of those needed for success in the other domains. (Gardner, 1993) One might possess the critical thinking and problem solving attributes necessary for one domain of intelligence, but lack some of the skills to succeed in other intelligences.

Each student possesses some degree of all nine intelligences. The goal should be to encourage students to effectively learn how to use all of the intelligences while at the same time allowing them to develop their own personal strengths. (Armstrong, 1994) Children who are encouraged to develop their talents become the people who most enjoy applying their competencies in challenging situations. (Csikszentmihalyi et al., 1993)

Furthermore, whenever an individual recognizes his or her abilities, talents, skills, and resources, then goes on to apply them in meaningful ways to meet challenges, that individual is raising his or her own competence level. (Mitchell, 1985)

In studies related to achievement and aptitude, Berliner and Biddle (1995) concluded that, regardless of what people claim about student characteristics, **opportunity** to successfully learn is the most powerful predictor of student achievement. Thus, the importance of utilizing the theory of multiple intelligence in the educational process of our children to create opportunities for them to excel is the most important thing that we can do as educators. By enabling children to learn through their own dominant intelligences we allow our students to feel that their success in the learning process was due to their own prowess. As a result, they want to continue learning and continue growing so they can develop as individuals. Success breeds success.

It is time that we stop teaching and remediating by our own personal standards of what intelligence means and allow our children to learn in the way they learn best! Give them that opportunity.

Dr. Gardner (1995) states that there is no single correct way to apply the construct of multiple intelligences to the classroom. Gardner (1993) believes the most productive human efforts result when individuals are engaged in numerous and diverse tasks which are meaningful, challenging, long-term, and complex.

Hands-on activities are favored by teachers who seek to generate interest in learning. (Zahorich, 1994) When students are deeply immersed in an interesting activity, they attain a heightened state of consciousness known as "flow." (Csikszentmihalyi, 1985) When this happens, the children lose track of time and want to continue with the activity even after the bell rings. They are thoroughly enjoying the learning process.

Teachers and parents should be encouraged to utilize teaching techniques which incorporate each of the nine intelligences. There are no "correct" ways to include the different intelligences into the learning process. One should incorporate the intelligences into assignments that best suit the individual student and that facilitate the learning of the particular goal/concept being introduced in class.

Figure 3.1 gives sample activities for each of the intelligences for each major grade level.

Figure 3.1

Sample activities which incorporate the nine intelligences:

Intrapersonal

Early Childhood

Tell "all about me" stories.

Draw "me" and family.

Prepare photo albums.

Think of a letter, and imagine how I would feel being the letter.

Tell a story from a "story starter" prompt.

Intermediate

Reflect in the mirror — who do I see?

Prepare a scrapbook of what influences me.

Write a story: "If I could be anything, what would I be and why?"

Explain how different physical activities make me feel.

Draw a picture of what "I" look like.

Middle School

Maintain a diary.

Pretend to be the author of a story and write about what I think he was feeling.

Prepare a self-progress chart.

Write a poem entitled "What I like about me."

Discuss how life would be different if I was born in another culture.

Secondary

Write an essay on "If I could start over, I would..."

Write a story about "What I want to achieve in the future."

Assess my strengths and weaknesses in different subject areas.

Maintain a portfolio.

Set short and long term goals.

Interpersonal

Early Childhood

Work with a friend putting a puzzle together.
Role-play different professions with a friend.
Discuss a favorite book with someone else.
Play noncompetitive games.
Work with a buddy to improve a skill.

Intermediate

Describe to a partner what I would do to solve a problem.

Role-play a character in a story.

Discuss the impact of a historical event on today's society.

Develop a "human" graph to see where people stand on an issue.

Analyze the moral of a story and discuss its impact on me.

Middle School

Draw a team logo.

Develop a team name.

Pretend to talk on cell phones to discuss the lessons.

Use creative problem solving/brainstorming.

Interview "someone in history" and give a report to the class.

Secondary

Complete a lesson using cooperative learning.

Use "jigsawing/expert groups" (each one learns a part and teaches the others).

Develop a group cheer.

Use lab teams to work on science projects.

Participate in a debate about a pertinent topic.

Naturalist

Early Childhood

"Play" outside/visit a park/walk on a nature trail.

Maintain an aquarium/terrarium.

Chart weather.

Classify food into the food pyramid.

Develop a "pet" zoo.

Intermediate

Take a nature walk.
Maintain a butterfly garden.
Study and taste food from different cultures.
Draw a map from my house to school.
Take care of a "classroom" pet.

Middle School

Prepare a nature guide.
Grow plants and maintain a log concerning
the growth/development.
Maintain a diary of the natural development of my body.
Collect stamps from around the world.
Understand the influences of nature on the weather.

Secondary

Develop a leaf collection.
Prepare a classification matrix.
Graph pro's and con's concerning a constitutional
amendment.
Answer story problems based on natural processes.
Write a story using vocabulary associated with nature.

Musical-Rhythmic

Early Childhood

Identify nature sounds.
Perform my favorite song/dance.

Play the keyboard to improve fine motor skills.

Create a song explaining how I am feeling.

Learn to use different instruments to keep a beat.

Intermediate

Make a recording of different classroom sounds.

Listen to different kinds of music from around the world.

Create a "radio show" to study a particular concept.

Use music as a mnemonic device.

Perform physical exercise to the beat of a song.

Middle School

Sing a "group" song.

Assign sounds to the different body parts.

Learn math concepts from musical beats and rhythms.

Recognize different pieces of technology via the sounds they make.

Illustrate a poem with appropriate music.

Secondary

Make musical instruments and compose a song.

Prepare a rap/song/jingle to assist in learning a particular lesson.

Learn about songs pertinent to different historical happenings.

Listen to "60 beats per minute" music in the classroom.

Watch films/movies and identify the importance the music had on the outcome.

Bodily-Kinesthetic

Early Childhood

Use sand tables/water tables to learn concepts.

Practice making letters on a salt tray.

Sort different shapes and colors.

Use magnetic letters to spell words.

Wear different costumes to understand different professions.

Intermediate

Play "Simon says" to assist with cross-lateral motion.

Play kick ball to learn spelling words.

"Act-out" the different parts of speech.

Walk the number line to learn math facts.

Pretend I am a particular person in a picture and "act-out" what I would be doing.

Middle School

Role- play different historical events.

Perform folk dances to learn about different cultures.

Add and subtract students to learn about fractions and equations.

Perform a drama on how a computer operates.

Develop a new game using content from a particular subject.

Secondary

Act out the meaning of a vocabulary word.

Perform a drama of a particular culture being studied.

Re-enact a battle of a particular war.

Visit an amusement park and study the physics involved in the different attractions.

Play charades to learn different concepts.

Visual-Spatial

Early Childhood

Explore painting with different mediums (fingers, feathers, crumpled paper, etc.)

Prepare pictures of oneself using items from a "junk box."

Learn words by playing "Pictionary."

Use bulletin boards to pique student interest.

Draw pictures of things seen under a microscope or through a telescope.

Intermediate

Draw a postage stamp of an historical era.

Draw a map of an ideal community.

Develop a bumper sticker about "Just Say No To…"

Pretend I am a person in the portrait, imagine what I am feeling.

Use highlighters to assist with reading a sentence.

Middle School

Prepare a cartoon strip explaining a short story.

Estimate measurements by sight.

Draw a poster summarizing an event.

Study a culture through its visual/graphic arts.

Develop a collage of different characters of a story.

Secondary

Prepare a mind map to summarize a story.

Develop a map out of clay.

Paint a mural of a history period.

Prepare a school survey and graph the results.

Prepare a web page.

Logical-Mathematical

Early Childhood

Use Legos to design and build things.

Use blocks to learn how to count and categorize.

Build a log home out of sticks and glue.

Make a calendar and keep it current.

Use a clock to tell time.

Intermediate

Have a race and play "math sprints" learning number values.

Teach how to use a calculator to solve problems.

Develop a "code" to decipher a "special" language.

Learn how to use measuring devices.

Predict how the story will end based on patterns of the book.

Middle School

Prepare a word search to learn key vocabulary words.

List examples where history repeated itself.

Prepare a time-line to student events in history.

Graph a math equation.

Develop a goal-setting chart in health/science.

Secondary

Play the stock market game in U.S. History and/or Economics.

Use brain-teasers to start the lesson.

Web attributes of different systems of the body.

Discover unknown entities in a math problem.

Play "guess the author" based on content from a story.

Verbal-Linguistic

Early Childhood

Record my favorite story on a C.D.

Listen to stories and songs on headphones.

Tell stories about my favorite activity.

Complete "word jumble" puzzles made with vocabulary words.

Create a puppet show about a story I heard.

Intermediate

Prepare a slogan that a historical figure could have used.

Play "What's My Line?" with different authors or characters of a story.

Write a "how-to" manual for keeping in good physical shape.

Compile a list of "school jokes."

Create a travel brochure of my favorite vacation spot.

Middle School

Write a campaign speech.

Produce a broadcast depicting different characters in a story.

Write a sequel to a story.

Write story problems for other students to solve.

Pick a destination and give directions on how to get there.

Secondary

Maintain a reflective journal.

Write a letter to the editor about a community problem.

Develop a "bag of knowledge" and present the information to the class.

Create a poem about myself.

Develop questions to answers provided about specific content areas.

Existential

Early Childhood

Paint me in the "middle" of my hobbies.

Role-play different professions.

Pick my favorite color and tell where I see it.

Tell what my favorite thing to do is to a friend.

Trace my family members' hands with mine in the middle of the picture.

Intermediate

Prepare a photo album with me in the center of the pages.

Visit museums to gain understanding of the world around me.

Write "pen-pals" from around the world.

Prepare a family tree.

Create a play about me and my friends.

Middle School

Participate in career day.

Maintain a journal of important events in my life.

Write a paper on why I am special.

Write a poem about what makes me unique.

Reflect on my life and how I am "feeling."

Secondary

Write my obituary establishing what I want society to remember about me.

Establish goals—both personal and school.

Job shadow someone in the profession that interests me.

Describe the places around the world that I want to visit and why.

Write a jingle about my life.

Figure 3.2

> **When planning a lesson, one can utilize the following key questions to determine the inclusion of the different intelligences.**

1. Logical-Mathematical: How can I include numbers, logic, and reasoning skills?

2. Verbal-Linguistic: How can I involve the written and spoken word?

3. Visual-Spatial: How can I use mental images, spatial displays, and color?

4. Musical-Rhythmic: How can I include music as part of the learning environment and incorporate emotional and inspired music into assignments?

5. Interpersonal: How can I involve students in cooperative groups and engage them in interpersonal skills?

6. Intrapersonal: How can I incorporate student feelings and allow for choice making?

7. Bodily-Kinesthetic: How can I incorporate bodily motions and one's capacity to handle objects skillfully?

8. Naturalist: How can I use relationships, awareness of species, and categorization?

9. Existential: How can I incorporate students' feelings about the world around them and enable them to see the big picture?

Figure 3.3

The steps that I use to create a multiple intelligence lesson plan include:

1. Focus on a specific objective or topic.

2. Ask the key multiple intelligence questions (see above).

3. Use creative problem solving to develop as many teaching/learning approaches as possible for each intelligence.

4. Establish a sequential plan.

5. Implement the plan.

6. Assess the outcome and begin planning once again.

Figure 3.4

Figure 3.4 lists sample products that can be developed/created from each intelligence.

Logical-Mathematical

pattern
chart
graph
mnemonic
outline
calculation processes

Verbal-Linguistic

poem

short story

news production

travel brochure

essay

Visual-Spatial

mind map

picture

poster

video

sculptures

collage

mural

Musical-Rhythmic

rap

cheer

jingle

dance

song

Interpersonal

debate

meeting

dialogue

cooperative learning activity

Intrapersonal

reflective journal

photo album

diary

autobiography

thinking log

Bodily-Kinesthetic

re-enactment

skit

charade

game

impersonation

Naturalist

classification
collection
species chart
nature walk
hands-on-lab
recording tape of environment sounds

Existential

journal

reflective writings

coaching assessment

self-portrait

Figure 3.5

One can also use the concept of multiple intelligences in behavior management. The information found here will give parents and teachers various ways to assist in getting a student's attention or teaching students rules and behavioral guidelines.

Verbal-Linguistic

Attention: Spoken; write on chart/board

Guidelines: Display written guidelines; verbally explain guidelines

Logical-Mathematical

Attention: Clock—time lost

Guidelines: Label each guideline and refer to the particular number

Visual-Spatial

Attention: Flicking lights; use stop light

Guidelines: Cartoon picture of guidelines

Bodily-Kinesthetic

Attention: Hold right hand-up

Guidelines: Use fingers to represent different guidelines; act out guidelines

Musical-Rhythmic

Attention: Tap a beat and have students repeat the beat

Guidelines: Sing a song orchestrating the guidelines

Interpersonal

Attention: Tell one person and he passes it on

Guidelines: Students discuss importance of guidelines

Intrapersonal

Attention: Pause; allow students to reflect and control themselves

Guidelines: Students reflect; journal about guidelines

Naturalist

Attention: Make an animal sound

Guidelines: Assign each guideline to a particular plant and/or animal

Existential

Attention: Put hand to chin indicating thought has been obtained

Guidelines: Students write how guidelines allow them to be a part of the class

Utilizing the multiple intelligences theory does work quite well. I have used it as a classroom teacher, parent, and college professor. Learning becomes real!

Incorporate these ideas and strategies and watch the children grow. Using the following hints, you will assist your children in "Discovering Excellence!"

Listed below are Doc's helpful hints relating to Multiple Intelligences. The hints are suggestions to improve teaching and to assist in the learning process.

DOC'S HELPFUL HINTS:

Use the multiple intelligence theory.

Make a concerted effort to utilize these strategies in your classroom. You will truly see a remarkable difference. Learning will become relevant and FUN! Both you and your students will enjoy the process.

Incorporate all nine intelligences in your teaching.

For maximum quality, one should strive to include all nine intelligences in the learning process. Most teachers tend to teach their classes using methods which reflect the way they themselves learn best. This is biased and unfair to many of their students. A good rule of thumb is to incorporate all the intelligences within a five-to-seven day period. This will provide each of your students with the opportunity to work outside of their dominant intelligence and enable each student to gain a better appreciation of all of the intelligences while at the same time giving each student opportunities to shine in his or her own domain.

The goal should be to encourage every student to learn using all nine intelligences but to also nurture his or her individual strengths. This process produces students who are "well-rounded" individuals.

Include as many intelligences as you can in each individual lesson.

Incorporating activities which involve three to four of the intelligences into a single lesson peaks a student's interest and adds diversity. Students are more apt to remain active participants in the process when each lesson incorporates more than one intelligence. These different activities also allow the teacher to include "state changes" in the lesson.

Be sure that the included activities fit the lesson plan. One shouldn't try to force an activity into a particular lesson in order to say that another intelligence was included. Pick activities that fit the lesson.

Create a risk-free environment in which students will feel free to try new activities.

Active, relevant learning tools will be new to some students. They might feel uncomfortable with the new activities at first and feel inhibited by the fear of failing. Students must be assured that it is okay to try new things and that it is okay to fail. *We all make mistakes.* We've all completed tasks that did not go quite as planned. *That is just fine!* Stress that these "failures" are just part of the learning process. Learning is a PROCESS. We all learn from our mistakes.

Include the different intelligences when you work with your child at home.

Home and school should be a partnership. If your child is struggling with a homework assignment, allow him or her to practice/use the information in the intelligence that makes the most sense to him or her at home. After the practice session, allow him or her to revisit the assignment and complete it as requested by the teacher.

Teach the child; do NOT remediate the student.

Instead of trying to remediate a struggling student with the same strategies that have given the student trouble thus far, enable the child to learn the information using his dominant intelligence. Teaching the student in the same way for an extended period of time will not produce the needed results. Enable students to develop their positive attributes, rather than forcing them to forever dwell on their weaknesses, lest they become discouraged and give up.

Allow students the opportunity to participate in all "specials."

Students need the opportunity to participate in the fine arts and the physical aspects of education. Children should be encouraged and given the chance to get involved in music, art, and physical education. Please do not punish a child by taking these classes away from him or her. Develop a different behavior management plan rather than denying these much needed opportunities to foster learning.

Schools in financial crisis need to develop other ways to save money rather than cutting their fine arts program. Research is overwhelming concerning the value a child receives in participating in the fine arts. Cognitive development is enhanced and ultimately student achievement is increased when students participate in the fine arts.

Allow your child to have FUN!

Learning should be FUN! Please let students learn in the way that they learn best. This process makes learning more enjoyable for everyone involved. Children are more apt to *want* to learn whenever they are enjoying the

PROCESS! Make learning something students want to do. Allow them to enjoy the PROCESS!

When one utilizes Doc's helpful hints, students are able to DISCOVER excellence through the use of a PERFECT process!

Chapter 4

Personal Power and Learned Helplessness

Personal Power and Learned Helplessness

"We will not lie, steal, or cheat, nor tolerate among us anyone who does. Furthermore, I resolve to do my duty and live honorably, so help me God."

United States Air Force Academy motto

The spirit of these words demands of us strength, courage, and dedication to a cause greater than ourself. The words are a statement of the most important single aspect of Academy life and they are at the center of a Cadet's core values.

"Duty, honor, country: Those three hallowed words reverently dictate what you ought to be, what you can be, what you will be. They are your rallying point to build courage when courage seems to fail, to regain faith when there seems to be little cause for faith, to create hope when hope becomes forlorn."

General of the US Army, Douglas MacArthur

These two quotes are well known, and truly taken to heart, by those disciplined soldiers who either have defended or are currently defending our great nation.

As a former social studies teacher and a former Army officer, these quotes remind me of the principles that our forefathers used when establishing this great nation. The personal integrity, responsibility and fortitude that they exhibited shines as an example to all Americans. We have all benefited from their efforts.

Putting others before self and sacrificing their personal ambitions for the ideals of democracy enabled those men to develop the necessary leadership skills needed to write a constitution that could guarantee Americans the freedoms that we enjoy today. All of the choices and liberties that we have today originated from the efforts of those responsible men. Where would we be if their ideals were replaced with *learned helplessness?*

People who learn to emulate good interpersonal skills are usually those who highly value a sense of integrity. They have learned to follow and emulate strong leaders out of an appreciation for their good qualities. A person has to learn how to follow and support good leaders before he or she can effectively lead an organization.

People with integrity are those that do what is *right* when other people are present. We often here that if one has integrity that he or she will do what is *right* when others are not around. I agree, but I also believe that peer pressure makes it much more difficult to do the *right* thing. It can be very difficult to do what you know is the correct thing in spite of the influence of your friends. Having good role models to emulate helps a person to distinguish between good and bad behavior while they are under the influence of their friends. Personal power must include personal integrity as part of its formula.

I have had the opportunity to travel the country as a consultant working with schools, businesses, and parent groups. As I have spoken with employers, I've noticed common themes in many of my conversations. Over and over again I have heard employers say, "We need people who can work well together, people who are disciplined, and people who have good interpersonal skills."

The overwhelming majority of companies have adopted the "team" concept. Employees who can work well with other employees on a designated team in order to get the job done are fast becoming a highly sought after commodity.

Unfortunately, according to business and industry leaders, most students leaving high school are lacking in these skills. Many graduates are not able to get along with others and do not possess the needed interpersonal skills to complete tasks either on their own or as part of a team without requiring constant prompting by their supervisors.

Diane Dodd-McCue prepared a summary of Ralph Kilmann's book, entitled Managing Beyond the Quick Fix, which was included in The Manager's Bookshelf — A Mosaic of Contemporary Views, edited by Jon Pierce and John Newstrom.

Kilmann points out that quick fixes do not produce lasting results. Success requires an integrated, holistic program and a lot of patience. He concludes that there are five tracks to organizational success. In order to plan out this integrated program, one must be able to schedule within and across the tracks. This demands coordination, sharing, and flexibility.

One of Kilmann's tracks is pertinent to this section of my book — that being *"The Team-Building Track."* This track focuses on three areas: managing troublemakers, team building, and inter-team building. Successful implementation of these characteristics creates a domino effect. When you curtail the disruptive behavior of troublemakers, others on the team will feel more comfortable and express themselves more freely. When the group can communicate freely it develops into a more effective team and work-related problems are more easily managed. When interconnected work groups become cooperative teams, organizational problems that span traditional group boundaries become more manageable. (Pierce & Newstrom, 1984)

Parents and teachers have a wonderful opportunity to assist in developing the skills needed for our children to function in this modern society and they should take full advantage of those opportunities. Students possessing the skills described by Ralph Kilmann are the ones who will be successful in meeting the challenges of the new work-force.

Aside from preparing our children to be successful in

their future jobs, developing effective interpersonal skills is necessary to ensure they can even function in their everyday lives. All of our children — preschool through high school — depend on these skills to get along with others. It is often assumed that these skills are developed in students simply by allowing them to interact between classes. Unfortunately, when viewing the statistics relating to school violence, gang activity, and children serving "correctional" time, it is obvious that these skills are lacking for many of our children. Teachers must make an effort if they expect children to develop these skills.

Hal Urban agrees that schools, for the most part, do a great job. But he points out that there is something missing in the curriculum. We do not teach children about life itself, about how it works, or about what the essentials are. People need assistance in learning the skills and developing the attitudes necessary to establish satisfying relationships, to set and achieve goals, and to feel good themselves. (Urban, 2003)

Students need to believe that they have the power to control their own destiny. A sense of "being in control" is needed for us to effectively overcome the daily situations that confront us. Human beings like to have input in the decision making process. Allowing students to make decisions at school and at home includes them in the formula that fosters "responsibility."

Ownership develops whenever one is given choices and allowed to determine which avenue to travel. In contrast, when students do not think that they have much control over their educational outcomes they tend to develop a sense of **"learned helplessness."** (Boggiano & Katz, 1991; Sedek & McIntosh, 1998)

Students begin to believe that they cannot be successful in the learning process. Excuse making begins to become the normal behavior. Teachers and parents begin to hear, *"I can't"* expressed by the child more often.

Once someone has internalized "learned helplessness" it is difficult to get that person to take on new challenges. A "defeated" attitude becomes evident in their outlook. The student stops believing that he or she can be successful in life and begins to make inappropriate choices. These students learn to expect others to do the work for them if it is to get done. Some of these students quit caring if the task is accomplished at all.

In the bestselling book entitled Fish, by Dr. Stephen Lundin, Harry Paul, and John Christensen, the authors address today's most pressing work issues and give solutions to the problems. They point out that successful companies hire employees that have chosen to love the work they do. These employees are able to *catch* the happiness, meaning, and fulfillment in their work every day. Employees are the ones who choose the attitudes they bring to work. A good employee brings a positive attitude.

The business that the authors referenced was Seattle's "Pike Place Fish." At the market, one finds employees who choose to have good attitudes. The employees at this business play. They have fun and enjoy their work. This creates energy. They include their customers in their good times. They enjoy making people happy. They are present at work — they are not thinking about being someplace else — they are mentally and emotionally at the job interacting with customers. (Lundin, Paul, & Christensen, 2000)

This successful fish market was able to eliminate the notion of "learned helplessness" and enable people to take control of their lives. These employees are feeling successful. This same feeling can happen in school as well. Students who are engaged in the classroom and actively involved in the learning process are going to demonstrate a feeling of personal power.

Whenever this type of environment is not present, unfortunate compensating behaviors begin to develop.

"Intellectual helplessness" is created in environments where poor instruction and inadequate learning strategies are the norm. (Sedek & McIntosh, 1998)

Teachers need to model good learning and teaching strategies. Students need to believe that if they put forth the effort that there will be a payoff. Smart work will be the norm once "learned helplessness" is eliminated. Students will choose to be "present" at school.

Students who have a sense of personal power tend to set higher goals for themselves. (Schunck & Zimmerman, 1996) Parents and teachers need to teach children how to establish realistic goals. Goals need to be personalized and have clarity. People need to have a specific target to shoot for or their efforts will be wasted on random or inappropriate pursuits. Our minds have a difficult time moving toward a generality. We need to review and revise our goals regularly.

Once students learn how to effectively set and use goals, their sense of **personal power** increases. They begin to believe that they are in control of their destiny.

Teachers need to allow students to have input in decision making. A sense of control over their lives produces a feeling of mastery. The opposite of mastery is helplessness. (Boggiano & Katz, 1991; Sedek & McIntosh, 1998)

I encourage teachers to include student input in developing classroom guidelines at the beginning of the school year. The guidelines should be worded in the positive rather than a list of "things not to do." We need to teach the behaviors we want; not the behaviors that we want to eliminate. The list should include no more than five to seven guidelines. Keep them positive and simple.

By allowing student input, **ownership** is fostered and their personal power is enhanced. The less adults depend upon dominance, threats, and punishments to control the environment, the more positive a student's attitude becomes and the higher a student's commitment to school work becomes. (Lunenburg & Schmidt, 1989)

Effective classroom management practices include encouraging children to take increasing responsibility for planning, organizing, and directing their learning. (Brophy, 1996) Teachers need to structure their classrooms and plan experiences that focus on the relationship between behavior and its consequences. By developing this structure, a child's sense of internal control is enhanced. (Nowicki & Barnes, 1973)

School personnel need to share the power. Whenever a teacher shares some of his or her power, the teacher actually becomes more powerful because students will understand that the teacher is simply adhering to the structure and not picking on any individual. They will more readily support a system they took part in building.

Giving students some of the power to choose causes personal power attributes to increase and learned helpfulness to dwindle.

As we handle personal power and learned helplessness issues more positively, schools will more often produce people that employers want working for them. Graduates will possess the needed interpersonal skills to be productive employees and to effectively function in relationships.

Listed below are Doc's helpful hints relating to Personal Power and Learned Helplessness. The hints are suggestions to improve teaching and to assist in the learning process.

DOC'S HELPFUL HINTS:

Treat children with respect and display integrity.

One should always be supportive of children in the learning process. The teacher/student relationship should never be adversarial but instead cooperative. Teachers and students should work together to establish classroom guidelines. The classroom environment should be one where adults and students have respect for one another and demonstrate integrity to each other. Treat others as you want to be treated.

Model good interpersonal skills for your children.

Actions speak louder than words. Teachers and parents need to be role models for the children. Using good interpersonal skills yourself reinforces to the children how important these skills are in communicating with others.

Teach the importance of and the "how to" of goal setting.

Instill in your children the importance of planning and establishing goals. Teach them that goals should be personalized. Time-lines should be included to assist with student accountability.

Use cooperative learning techniques in your teaching repertoire.

Cooperative learning techniques teach the pertinent subject matter along with an interpersonal skill. A child's personal power is greatly enhanced when taught by a teacher using this teaching strategy.

Foster an atmosphere where cooperation is the norm.

The typical classroom centers on competition – the students are competing for a particular grade or goal. Some competition in the classroom is good but cooperation should be included as well. A cooperative classroom creates a win/win environment for everyone.

Enable your students to plan, organize, and direct their own learning.

Children need to take an active role in the learning process. They should not depend on the teacher to do all of the work. Learning becomes relevant whenever the students help orchestrate the process themselves.

Collaborate with children in establishing classroom guidelines.

Cooperatively, teachers and students should develop four to five social guidelines. Students will accept the guidelines and put forward a concerted effort to make them work since they helped establish them. The traditional "list of rules" that teachers demand of students places the burden of classroom management on the teacher alone rather than involving the students.

The guidelines should be positive statements that allow the children to know the expected behaviors. We need to stress the behaviors that we want; not those that we do not want.

Instill the importance of choosing a positive attitude.

We cannot always control what happens to us but we can control how we respond to it. Children need to learn how to remain positive even in adverse conditions. One can be a perfect one just as he or she can be a perfect ten!

Do not accept "I can't" statements from students.

Teach students that *"can't"* never did anything. Remind children that whenever they say, *"I can't,"* what they are really saying is, *"I choose not to."* Foster an *"I can"* attitude that facilitates a risk-free environment.

Allow children to follow as well as lead.

All good leaders learned how to follow prior to leading others. Provide opportunities for all students to follow and emulate the good qualities in others and to internalize this very important skill.

Build a sense of trust in your children.

Trust is a vitally important life skill. It is a virtue. We need to be able to trust, follow and learn from other people in order to succeed. As teachers we must model both trust and trustworthiness. One should be just as good as his word. Children respect people whom they can trust.

Be honest and establish believability.

Adults need to be honest with children. They should not "stretch the truth" either to make themselves look better or to "sugar-coat" a problem. Children are more apt to take risks in the learning process whenever the teacher is believable and honest.

When one utilizes Doc's helpful hints, students are able to DISCOVER excellence through the use of a PERFECT process!

Chapter 5

Doc's "Guiding Principles"

Doc's "Guiding Principles"

I have had the good fortune of experiencing many things during my life. Having served as a military officer, classroom teacher, coach, principal, professor, and consultant, I have many valuable experiences from which to glean my ideas concerning responsibility. I have found that there are certain attributes which must be developed in order for one to become a responsible individual. This chapter is devoted to my basic beliefs concerning the development of those attributes.

On the following pages of this chapter, you will find my *guiding principles* and a summary of each.

Everything is PERFECT!

Every morning affords us opportunity. New challenges await us in every day. We cannot control what hand life will deal us but we can control how we respond to each situation. In order to become "well-rounded" individuals we must learn to respond appropriately in both the good times and the challenging times.

Learn to picture life as a continuum. On the far left side is a 1 — one of the worst days of your life — and on the far right side is a 10 — one of the best days of your life. You can be a "perfect" 1 just like you can be a "perfect" 10! Rise to the challenge! Your positive attitude will attract others.

Learn to live life one day at a time and stop worrying about the things you cannot control. The *"everything is perfect"* attitude is contagious. If your children act disrespectfully, it is perfect. If your students fail to turn in homework, it is perfect. These experiences give us feedback to create the perfect learning experiences.

We can enable students to learn from their lack of responsible behavior. It is okay to make mistakes. We learn from our mistakes and move to new heights. Enjoy your family, friends, co-workers, and life —see everything as being PERFECT!!

Process produces the Product.

Everything we do in life is ongoing — it is cyclical. We never "get there." As soon as our children complete a task, we are reevaluating to see where improvements can be made. Nothing remains constant. The one certainty that we have in life is that there is going to be change. Life is a process. We should constantly be creating the necessary environment to allow positive changes to occur.

Teaching students to try to understand why something happened is much more important than having them simply observe and repeat the correct answer. Understanding the process involved enables a student to replicate that process and use it in order to face future challenges that may confront him or her. Focusing on the process assists us in discovering excellence.

Attitude defines the individual.

Children have a choice to make every time they confront a new situation. Do they see the cup as half full or half empty? People who view life through a positive lens generally experience a healthier and happier life.

Others are attracted to people who have a "can do" attitude. People who view challenges in a positive light tend to be successful in overcoming them. They do not let adversity get the best of them.

Many of our greatest historical figures had to overcome tremendous adversity in their lives. The following are some of the more famous examples.

Overcoming Adversity:

Einstein was 4 years old before he could speak.

Beethoven's music teacher once said of him "as a composer he is hopeless."

When *Thomas Edison* was a boy his teacher told him that he was too stupid to learn anything.

Michael Jordon was cut from his high school basketball team.

A newspaper editor fired *Walt Disney* because he thought he had no good ideas.

Winston Churchill failed the 6th grade.

Steven Spielberg dropped out of high school in his sophomore year and was persuaded to come back to school. After being placed in a learning-disabilities classroom, he lasted a month and dropped out of school again forever.

Obviously, these people had a choice to make. They chose to make the best of life. As a result they overcame adversity, and went on to become successful.

Less is more.

Does spending more days at school assure quality learning? Does assigning more homework assure better understanding? I don't think so. More is not necessarily better. More is just more! By concentrating on smaller chunks of information, students can usually reach a greater understanding. Taking on too many tasks usually results in the student only partially completing the objective. We can get more in-depth by concentrating our efforts on less.

Students must be given enough information in an assignment in order to determine what items need to be studied in-depth and to begin establishing priorities and agendas for themselves. This develops a realistic sense of responsibility in our students. They begin to realize that they cannot be everything to all people. They will learn to evaluate their assignments and concentrate on the most important material.

Allow your students to be involved in choosing what they undertake and encourage them to do it correctly. My father always told me, "If you are going to do something, do it right, or don't do it at all." Doing one thing right is better than partially competing several tasks.

Actions equal choice.

A picture is worth a thousand words. And so it is with our actions. The way we conduct ourselves leaves a lasting impression. Children will remember the way we acted long after they have forgotten what we said.

Once students establish goals for themselves, the manner in which they pursue those goals will determine the amount of success they will achieve. The choices the student makes will determine the outcome of his or her efforts. If all the student has learned from us is information and jargon then he or she won't have the necessary skills to implement his or her plan. They must see us model the method. They must be allowed to take part in the process themselves as well. Actions speak louder than words.

A good rule to live by is as follows: Once you have chosen to undertake something, pretend you'll be signing the end product. Keeping in mind that your actions will reflect on you personally, you are much more likely to give your best and most concerted effort.

Knowledge produces wisdom.

Having an understanding of our past will assist us as we head into the future. Students must be able to analyze their past experiences and draw lessons from them in order to gain wisdom that they can apply in the future. The fundamental lessons of life are the foundation of all future learning. Learning to glean lessons from past experiences and apply that knowledge to the future is what grants us wisdom.

Knowledge is the lowest level of learning on Bloom's Taxonomy. By integrating knowledge with Bloom's upper levels — application, analysis, synthesis, and evaluation — students are able to become very wise. The choices they make will be based on factual information; not just on their notions.

The wise student builds life on solid ground. Obtaining wisdom allows children to be responsible citizens who make good choices as they interact with others.

Smart work builds success.

In order to be successful, our students must develop a strong work ethic. I don't necessarily believe long hours are required in order to create productive work habits. Students do need to take their assigned tasks seriously and put forth the necessary time and effort but there is a difference between *hard work* and *smart work.* Though it is true that practice is necessary, only perfect practice brings perfect results.

Sometimes students find themselves working very hard for extended periods of time without accomplishing much of anything — they are spinning their wheels. Letting a student continue to struggle for an extended period of time doesn't guarantee positive results. In fact, it will very likely frustrate the student and rob him or her of the will to engage in such activities again.

I contend that it is more beneficial for students to learn how to study a situation, determine a game plan, and *work smart* in a productive manner toward accomplishing their goals than it is for them to struggle on their own without the proper guidance. A little coaching can be much more helpful than hours of struggle. Efficient work strategies must be learned before they can be applied. Take the time to help your students learn smart work habits.

Honesty is the best thing.

At the beginning of chapter four, I quoted the United States Air Force Academy's honor code. It states, "We will not lie, steal, cheat nor tolerate among us anyone who does." The cadets at the Air Force Academy truly live by this code. Responsible people always value honesty as one of the highest virtues we have. It takes a person with character to tell the truth even when it might hinder the success of his or her proposal.

When you are honest with your students they will begin to emulate you. Honesty develops trust. People feel comfortable around those they trust. Students are much more apt to take risks in the learning environment when trust has been created.

Telling the truth to your students also allows them to have a clear vision of the path down which they are headed. It gives them the big picture.

Give credit where it belongs.

Those who possess personal power and good interpersonal skills know how to be part of a team. As a coach, I tried to instill in the athletes the importance of teamwork. When you are part of a team, it is important that your priorities center on the good of the team rather than promoting yourself.

General George C. Marshall once said, "There's no limit to the good you can do if you don't care who gets the credit." Responsible students will do good things just because they recognize that those things should be done. Make sure you don't overlook these students when it comes time to distribute rewards.

Students shouldn't be allowed to take credit for doing something that they did not accomplish. That is just as bad as lying or stealing. Though credit can be stolen, excellence can only be developed honestly.

Excellence requires sacrifices.

"No pain; no gain" is a very popular saying in the world of sports. The translation means, "excellence requires sacrifices." In order to reach our goals, we have to *work smart* and make sacrifices along the way.

This generation of students lives in a society that promotes instant gratification. As a result, it is difficult to convince our young people to make sacrifices for future gains. Our students want results to come *easy* and they want them **NOW.**

Credit card companies use this concept to their advantage in their advertisements by encouraging young people to *buy now – pay later.* This is just backwards. Why pay interest on your spending to a credit card company when you could earn interest on your savings in a checking account?

Students discovering excellence know that the best way to go is *pay now – play later!* I like to call this plan the *self-control* or *self-discipline* plan. Everything that is worth having is worth waiting for. Setting lofty goals and being disciplined enough to make the necessary sacrifices will pay big dividends in the end.

Students need to keep in mind that they may have to be willing to give up some things now in order to obtain something better in the future.

Determination produces results.

We are given many opportunities during our lives. We all make choices each and every day. We see a fork in the road and we choose which path to travel. Once a road is selected, we may experience bumps, pot holes, and detours. If we are determined to reach the end of the road, we will find ways to handle all of the setbacks that come our way.

Our students must learn that *determination* is what will allow them to become successful. Positive results don't just happen — we have to make them happen. Students need to be determined to make the temporary sacrifices needed in order to obtain long lasting results. Setting goals, developing a game plan, and then carrying out the plan is the process that enables all of us to experience success. Determination produces long range results!

Self-confidence opens doors.

In order for our children to have personal power they must first begin to believe in themselves. When a child's self-esteem is high, the child becomes willing to pursue new challenges and open new doors. When a child experiences some success, the child becomes confident that he or she can do it again. As I said before, success breeds success.

Humility builds character.

It is important for students to realize that they are no better or worse than anyone else. Society is a team and it takes every member doing his or her best for that team to be a success. When our talents are pooled together, a great deal of success can be realized in our communities.

When a student begins to value his or her neighbor and understand that one's success depends on learning to cooperate and work together in teams then humility and character begin to replace selfishness and arrogance.

As a teacher, when you are humble and gracious toward others your students will begin to emulate you. Give credit where credit is due. Praise others for their efforts. Acknowledge the successes of those around you.

Flexibility improves creativity.

Learning to make plans and follow through with them is an essential skill for students to learn in order to remain headed in the right direction. However, sometimes they will experience unexpected setbacks. They must have the ability to be flexible in order to overcome these challenges. Critical thinking skills and problem solving skills are very important for our children to develop. All children need to learn to become more creative. They should have opportunities to come up with their own solutions to setbacks.

As parents and teachers, we have the awesome responsibility of teaching and modeling these guiding principles to our children. Once our children internalize these ideals, their lives will be so much more enjoyable and productive. They will become more responsible and they will make good choices. Their responsible actions will allow them to be productive citizens and to get along well with their peers and their supervisors.

Chapter 6

Responsibility Strategies

Responsibility Strategies

Wouldn't it be nice if every student entering our classrooms took responsibility for their own actions? Wouldn't it be nice if every student made good choices? Wouldn't it be nice if every student had a positive attitude? Wouldn't it be nice if every student studied and took learning seriously? Wouldn't it be nice if every student was committed to excellence?

Unfortunately, many of our children will not possess the attributes needed to be responsible students when they enter our classrooms. This chapter offers ideas to assist parents and teachers in fostering responsibility in our children.

Developing responsible children is a process. There is not a quick fix available. Please try these strategies and enjoy the results.

Doc's helpful strategies

Provide Choices.

People have a basic need to feel free and independent. When students don't believe that this need is being met, they may lose their motivation to learn. (Rogers, Ludington, Graham, 1999)

One of the biggest mistakes that teachers and parents can make is to allow our children to become accustomed to letting others make their choices for them. (Urban, 2003) When children aren't involved in decisions, *learned helplessness* becomes incorporated into their personality. We need to provide choices to our students and encourage independent thought.

We have numerous opportunities to allow our students to make their own choices in the classroom. Here are some examples:

Let students answer either the even or odd numbered questions on a quiz.

Give students two choices on how make-up work will be completed.

Let students decide whether to outline the chapter or complete a graphic organizer.

Let students choose the topic for the report.

Let students choose what kind of writing utensil to use.

Let students select what intelligence to use when completing the project.

Create a risk-free environment.

Students need to know that it is okay to make mistakes. In fact, they need to know that making mistakes is part of the learning process. Everyone makes mistakes. We want to encourage children to try new things — to be an "active" component in the process of learning.

Whenever we work in the upper levels of Bloom's Taxonomy, we apply knowledge and develop critical thinking skills. When students use application, analysis, synthesis, and evaluation processes it opens the door for them to try new things — to apply information to a "new setting." In doing this, mistakes will be made. It is okay.

Thank students for taking risks and encourage them to use their mistakes as learning tools. Encourage students to try new things and reward them when they do.

When calling on students for an answer, give them the option to pass on a particular question if they don't know the answer. When a student is called upon and says "I pass" then the teacher should call on someone else. This takes the pressure off of the student. We have all had a situation in which our mind went blank and we could not think of the correct response. If the teacher keeps asking the student for an answer and/or makes a negative comment about the student for not knowing the answer, the student can become embarrassed and sometimes angry. When that happens, the student's brain begins to shut down. The learning environment has become *brain-antagonistic.* Use the "I pass" strategy to create a risk-free environment.

Use "Freedom Phrases."

Chic Moorman, author of Spirit Whispers, writes about giving choices to our students. Chic says that there are three words that assist students in becoming aware of their responsibility for creating reactions to events. Those three words are "choose," "decide," and "pick." We need to allow students to choose, decide, and pick from their options after explaining what the consequences of each option are.

Teachers and parents should not be making all of the decisions for our students. When we do, those decisions remain OUR decisions; not the decisions of the children. Chic points out that we should give the scenario and then let the student select the answer. (Moorman, 2001)

Some examples of "Freedom Phrases" that we can use to encourage our students to make good decisions:

Student: May I go to the restroom?
Teacher: If you can go and be back before class begins. You decide.

Student: May I write about this topic?
Teacher: If it will meet the objective of the
assignment. You decide.

Student: Do I have to answer all of the assigned
problems?
Teacher: If you can answer some of the problems and
have a clear understanding of the objective
then go ahead. You pick the problems.

According to Mr. Moorman, Freedom Phrases include:

"It is up to you."
"You Choose."
"You decide."
"You make that decision."
"I am comfortable with whatever you decide."

Look for the candy.

Is the cup half full or half empty? Is the cookie jar half
full or half empty? Is the bag of candy half full or half
empty? It is all subject to interpretation — it is how we
view things — it is our attitude.

Many of us have a tendency to look for the negatives
rather than the positives. You get what you ask for –
whenever you expect and look for negative behavior in
your students then that is what you'll get.

Children need to be taught to look for the opportunity
before them, rather than dwelling on what they are
missing. They cannot control everything that happens to
them at home or at school but they can control how they
react to the situation. Remind children to look for the
candy instead of pouting because the bag is half empty.
When they learn to value the opportunities before them,
they will gain a useful skill that they can use in life.
Having a positive outlook will open new doors of
opportunity to them.

Define meaningful expectations.

Students need to know exactly what you expect of them. Expectations should be made clear and simple. Prior to beginning an assignment, teachers need to make sure that the students understand the purpose of the activity, what the end product should be at the conclusion of the project, and they need to make sure that the students have been provided with easy to follow step-by-step instructions.

It is difficult to hit a moving target so make sure your expectations remain consistent. Use examples, post guidelines, write out helpful hints, and use any other tools that will make your expectations clear. Do not assume that everyone understands your expectations – make sure they do. Also, be sure to model and demonstrate what you expect from them when you ask for "quality work."

Expect accountability.

Children need to understand *cause and effect* relationships. Once you clearly inform children of the goals and objectives that pertain to them, make sure you continue to observe their progress until completion. Your students must be held accountable for their progress.

Teachers should instill in their students a firm grasp of the concept that *for every action there is a reaction.* Students need to be taught that every choice they make has a consequence. In your class, make sure that they receive the consequences that were predetermined.

Remember that children tend to follow guidelines that they helped develop better than rules demanded of them by the teacher. Involving your students in a collaborative effort to set up guidelines and consequences for their own behavior will assist in developing an atmosphere of accountability in the classroom.

Make sure children understand the consequences of not following through with responsibilities. Consequences can be used to motivate students best when they are respectful, seen as a choice, related, and planned.

Be firm, fair, and consistent.

Responsibility is fostered when love and respect are apparent. Be sure to be involved in the children's lives, let them know that you believe in them, and use praise regularly. In addition to love and respect, there are three other attributes needed for improving a student's responsibility. These attributes are: *be firm, be fair, and be consistent.*

Be firm: Use a good balance between being too easy and too tough. You must be in control but you must also be willing to listen. Children need an adult who will help "draw the line" but they also need an adult who is open to suggestions.

Be fair: Be sure everyone receives the same consequences. Do not bend the rules for some of your students. Students will adhere to guidelines if they believe they are fair, but are apt to break rules they see as unfair.

Be consistent: Adults need to use consistency when disciplining children. Teachers must follow the same guidelines and administer the same consequences every time a particular situation arises. Do not let children convince you that the consequence is not necessary in a particular occasion. Teachers need to be sure to use the same *cause and effect* relationships every day and in every class. Without consistency, children become confused and deprived of the opportunity to learn some of life's greatest lessons.

Develop organizational skills.

Being organized is one of the attributes associated
with self-discipline. A self-disciplined student will likely be
more responsible and organized in his or her efforts. We
need to encourage our students to become more
organized and show them how. Some tools that can help
build organizational skills in students are:

Checklists

Assignment books

Routines (developed by both the teacher and the
student)

Completed assignment charts

Priority lists

Plan books

Neatness and organization in the classroom

Deciding together where things belong

Develop goals.

All of our achievements originated as goals. A
successful person sets goals which chart a path to where
the person wants to go. Success does not happen by
accident. We make it happen.

Hal Urban points out that living your life without goals is
like taking a journey without knowing where you are
headed. If you don't know your destination, you will
probably get *nowhere.* You do not have to select the
correct path in order to get nowhere. Any road will get
you there as long as you neglect setting specific goals for
yourself. (Urban, 2003)

We need to teach students how to write specific goals.
Their goals need to have dates attached to them and

they should be regularly reviewed and revised. Have students celebrate their successes along the way. Once a particular goal has been reached, a final celebration should be had and a new, measurable goal established. Be sure the students establish realistic goals.

Be a role model.

Teachers should be sure that their behavior is responsible — students are watching. I have always stressed to teachers that we should model the behavior we want; not the behavior that we do not want. Our actions speak louder than our words. Teachers and parents need to maintain a positive attitude and demonstrate responsible behavior in everything they do.

Use guest speakers to assist in the modeling process. One can also have students read about people who are worth emulating.

As adults, we need to model the golden rule: "do unto others as you would have them do unto you."

Use demonstrations.

Sometimes "good" directions are still confusing to some students. Some of your students will be visual learners instead of auditory learners. Teachers can assist students in understanding the directions for a particular task by demonstrating how to do it themselves.

Active, hands-on learning is a wonderful teaching methodology. Examples and demonstrations are very helpful in eliminating confusion in the classroom.

Methods of demonstration:

Working a sample problem on the board
Completing a mind map
Setting your own goals
Preparing products related to each intelligence
Modeling responsible actions

Attitude Adjusters

Along with these helpful hints, I have successfully used *attitude adjusters* in developing responsible students. These easy to use skills truly assist students get in touch with the positive power they have over how they feel, think, and act. Once students learn these skills, they can consciously influence the events in their lives and produce the desired results. Some of the following information has been adapted from Chick Moorman's book, Spirit Whisperers. (2001, Personal Power Press)

1. "Dog" statements.

"Dog" statements are verbal responses that students can use to reverse the negative vibes sent their way through harsh words, put-downs, sarcasms, or criticism. Just as a dog fetching a thrown stick brings it back to the owner, a student collects this negative energy and returns it back to the sender.

By transforming this negative energy into a positive situation, the child can more easily maintain a positive mental state. It benefits a student to learn not to take offense but instead return the communication to the sender in a way that does not contain negative energy.

If a student hears someone say, "girls are not very smart in math," the *dog statement* response could be, "Girls do very well in math" or "There are several prominent female mathematicians."

2. Flip the page.

A second "attitude adjuster" is *flip the page.* This is a symbolic gesture that reminds children that the past is over and the present situation is where their personal power is needed. Whenever something from the past is bothering a student, have the student reflect on it and write it down on a piece of paper. Once the student is finished, tell him or her to turn the page over. In doing so, the student will see a blank piece of paper — a clean slate.

Whenever students use this "attitude adjuster" they are able to leave the past behind. One cannot do anything about what happened in the past. Students should be encouraged to look to the future. They can control their own destiny by using their positive energy rather than dwelling on the negative.

3. Twist and shout.

Twist and shout is an "attitude adjuster" which is similar to *flip the page.* Students are encouraged to write their frustrations out on sticky notes. Once completed, have each student stand and place the note on their hip and "twist" until the note falls to the ground.

Once the paper has fallen to the floor, the student should consider his or her frustration gone — it is out of his or her mind. With the negative energy gone, your students can devote their energies to important things facing them. This exercise can also be done mentally.

4. Develop a slogan.

Another exercise that teachers can use is *develop a slogan.* The students should be asked to develop a slogan that will help motivate them. Teachers can have students assess the situation at hand, brainstorm, and develop a slogan that exemplifies what it is they want to accomplish. Students should put the slogan into action whenever the time is appropriate. Examples include: Aim high!; Be all that you can be!; Don't try—just do it!; I don't settle for second best!; and Stand back! Learning is taking place here!

5. Quote a quote.

Yet another "attitude adjuster" is *quote a quote.* Have your students collect quotes from friends, family members, and/or famous people. Allow students to share a quote a day and then place them on a display board. Also, allow students to develop their own original quotes for the board. Hearing and seeing several positive quotes encourages students to remain positive. These quotes will assist students discover excellence!

6. Grill it.

Grill it is an "attitude adjuster" similar to *flip the page* and *twist and shout.* Have a student write his or her problems on a piece of paper, then place the paper into a grill. Once the paper has caught fire and disintegrated, remind the student that the problems have disappeared just like the paper. They are no longer with us — they are gone. This exercise reminds students that life goes on. Once our problems are placed in the past, our future can afford us a bright new beginning.

7. CPT Kirk

CPT Kirk is an "attitude adjuster" generated from the movie Star Trek. CPT Kirk, one of the characters in the movie, was living in *cosmic time.* This exercise enables students to choose their point of perspective.

The *CPT Kirk* exercise reminds children to back up and look at a situation from a different perspective. A student sometimes needs to mentally back up and look at a situation from the vantage point of one or two years in the future. *How important will this event be?* Then have them step back even further — ten to twenty years into the future. *Will this event be important to you at that time?*

The CPT Kirk concept of time allows students to make the rationalization that the issues which may seem extremely important at the moment might seem much less significant as time progresses. A tough situation will pass. Time heals all wounds. Children can learn to control their destinies by controlling their perspectives.

8. "I" can.

Another "attitude adjuster" is *"I" can.* All too often students will respond to a request, "I will try." Try is not a positive word. It gives students "wiggle room." They have an *out.* If they do not follow through and complete the task, they can still say that they tried.

Normally, people who say, "I will try" do not have the intention of really completing the task in mind. It's just a nice way of saying that they will not be getting the task accomplished.

Have your students say, **"I can"** do it. That is a positive statement that leads to positive results. When the students believe that they can accomplish the assigned task, that assists them in accomplishing their goals. The power of positive thinking is awesome. Once a student feels he or she can do it, the best effort will be given.

Incorporate these "attitude adjusters" into your teaching repertoire. They are simple to administer. The results will enable students to become responsible people with a strong sense of personal power.

Chapter 7

Motivation

Motivation

Society is filled with negativity. Listen to the news, read the papers, listen to people discuss politics, and you'll hear a lot of the negatives in life. I contend that we should focus on the numerous positive things happening to us as well. People are doing good things. We need to reward excellence and focus on the positive rather than look for the "foul-ups." John Dewey said, "A great society not only searches out excellence, but rewards it when it is found." By rewarding excellence, we can improve a child's motivation to discover excellence.

There are numerous definitions and ideas pertaining to the topic of motivation. Many inspirational quotes stem from this concept.

"It's important to remember that every person is different and has to be motivated differently."
- Coach Mike Krzyzewski

"If you always do what you always did, you'll always get what you always got." - Verne Hill

"The worst possible mistake you can make is to be constantly fearful you will make one."
- Anonymous

"Leadership is the quality that transforms good intentions into positive actions; it turns a group of individuals into a team." - T. Boone Pickens

"Opportunity often goes unrecognized because it wears overalls and often looks like work.
- Anonymous

"Get a good idea and stay with it. Dog it, and work at it until it's done, and done right." - Walt Disney

"The important thing in this world is not where we stand, but in what direction we move." - Goethe

"We must not... ignore the small daily differences we can make which, over time, add up to be big differences." - Marian Wright Edelman

"A diamond is a lump of coal that stuck with it."
- Anonymous

"Luck is what happens when preparation meets opportunity." - Vince Lombardi

"Failure is only the opportunity to begin again more intelligently." - Henry Ford

"Learning is the discovery that something is possible." - Fritz Perl

"Even if you're on the right track, you'll still get run over if you just sit there." - Will Rogers

"Success is peace of mind, which is a direct result... [of] knowing you did your best to become the best thing you are capable of becoming."
- John Wooden

"We can learn something new anytime we believe we can." - Virginia Satir

"It's never too late — in fiction or in life — to revise." - Nancy Thayer

Motivation is the internal drive to have one's needs met. The word *motivation* comes from the root word *motive,* which Webster defines as "the sense of need, desire, etc. that prompts an individual to act." Our motives and desires come from within us; therefore, no one else can control them. Motivation is unique to each individual.

Parents and teachers can assist in the process of enabling children to attain the desire and belief that they can be successful by rewarding their efforts. Whenever someone experiences some success, it motivates that person to increase his or her efforts to attain the results needed in order to have continued success in that particular field or setting. Past success develops future motivation! Success breeds success.

We can measure the balance of our motivation by answering three questions.

1. Do I have the required "want," "desire," and "need" to attain my goal?

2. Do I have the perseverance (stick-to-it'ness) to accomplish it?

3. Do I have a clear mental picture (mental imagery) of myself accomplishing it?

One has to have a desire to set motivation in motion. One has to want something. When the desire is evident, one will apply the needed effort to try to obtain the goal. Desire is the attribute that all highly successful people have.

An important characteristic of desire is commitment. If the commitment is present, one will invest the time and practice needed to accomplish the task.

One needs to be able to "see" success. Visualization is so very important. A clear mental picture is needed in order to accomplish the task and to stay motivated.

The brain does not know the difference between the conscious and the subconscious. If you visualize yourself being successful at an activity, your mind counts that as a positive experience.

Albert Einstein said that the true genius is the person who has mastered the art of visualization. One needs to experience the feat in the "mind's-eye" in order to carry out the success in real life.

Athletes have used this concept for decades. Tiger Woods discusses this idea in his book, How I Play Golf, which was published in 2001. Tiger states that he watches videos of both himself and others who have won the Master's Tournament before going out to play in it. In his mind's eye he watches himself accomplish something prior to actually doing it physically.

Dr. Charles Garfield has studied the habits of high achievers for many years. In his book, Peak Performers, he writes that all high achievers have the ability to imprint images of successful actions in their minds. They mentally practice the specific behaviors and skills necessary to reach their intended outcomes. (Urban, 2003)

You have to believe in yourself in order to become a success. The *belief* that you can accomplish a task is foundational when you are seeking to motivate yourself. One will not continue investing as much effort into trying to accomplish an objective if one does not believe that it can be completed.

A student's assigned tasks need to be manageable. Therefore, all classroom assignments should be individualized. Teachers and parents need to make sure the task will be beneficial for the student. They also need to ensure that the task is manageable, worthwhile, and purposeful.

As students accomplish the goals, the parents and teachers need to "reward excellence"—affirm that the job was done well!

"Rewarding Excellence" is the key to motivation. Affirmation is the key ingredient in "Rewarding Excellence." Affirmation means searching for and locating the good in people. It includes encouragement, praise, *feedforward statements*, applause, and supporting others. A student's belief that he or she can succeed is greatly enhanced by all of the attributes of affirmation. The remainder of this chapter will deal with "affirming others."

"Rewarding Excellence"

Students need encouragement. Encouragement leads to intrinsic motivation. Using positive verbal feedback produces an increase in intrinsic motivation. (Ryan & Deci, 2000; Tang & Sarsfield-Baldwin, 1991)

The reverse is true as well. Negative verbal feedback decreases one's intrinsic motivation and persistence. (Friedman & Lackey, 1991)

We need to praise children for their hard work and effort rather than just focusing on their intelligence. Praise for ability rather than for effort diminishes effort after failure, creates less enjoyment in the learning process, and lowers the performance level. (Mueller & Dweck, 1998)

Major themes of an encouraging environment include:

The belief that all children can learn.

Each person is a unique individual.

The environment is positive.

Teachers and parents believe that children are capable of learning.

We need to focus on each of these encouraging statements. Most children enter the school system with the desire to please us – yearning for the opportunity to learn. Unfortunately, due to many factors, this attitude changes for many of them. Some children lose their love for learning by the time they graduate from high school. It is vitally important that we provide as MUCH encouragement as possible when they enter the school system and ensure that this *encouraging process* continues throughout their scholastic careers.

Students who receive encouraging comments on their papers raise their assessment scores to a larger degree than students receiving no comments. Criticism is found to be counterproductive. (Page, 1958) Positive comments on papers have been found to increase subject interest (Butler & Nisan, 1986) and intrinsic motivation. (Cameron & Pierce, 2002)

Examples of encouraging statements include:

Demonstrate how you think it could be done.

Your hard work really stands-out in this project.

The project is good. Your hard work is showing.

Please check your work. You will know whether you need more information to complete the assignment.

How do you think you did on this mind-map?

Your participation helped clarify the point.

Your are off and running. Please review to see what modifications you need to make.

Examples of discouraging statements include:

You are doing a good job, BUT…

I can't believe that you can't do it.

WOW! Look at all of those mistakes.

Susan can do it. Why can't you?

Do you ever listen to anyone?!?

I've told you 100 times this would happen.

Why can't you be like your brother/sister?

If you don't change your ways, you are going to fail.

Get up! You aren't hurt.

Are you a little sissy?

You won't believe what I heard about you.

What am I going to do with you?

I'm ready to give up on you!

Let me do that for you.

You are wrong.

I truly believe in praise. We all like to hear that we are doing well. Praise should be given regularly and in conjunction with appropriate *feedforward* comments.

Teachers and parents need to focus on praising the qualities and behaviors that the child values. Praise should be individualized. What one person likes and enjoys receiving could very well be different than what "feels" good to someone else. By knowing our children, we can use the "right" kind of praise to assist with their intrinsic motivation.

We need to consider the child's personal needs when praise is given so that we give it in the manner most beneficial to him or her. Some people want to receive praise in private and away from their peers. Others need public recognition.

Also, make it genuine. If everyone receives the same praise for different levels of accomplishment, it may lose its effectiveness. We can give non-judgmental praise by stressing the specific characteristics that the person performed rather than just praising the individual. (e.g., "I see you have all of your materials and are on time for class.") Just use common sense. Give praise that is sincere and preferably one-on-one.

We need to model our passion for learning to our students. We can live our lives in such a way that our children know we are lifelong learners and that we look at life through positive lenses. One can display affirmation in the classroom. Place the charts and posters high on the wall to promote recall.

Example affirmations include the following:

Aim high!

Soar with the falcons!

Just do it!

I think I can; therefore, I know I can.

Set your eyes on success.

Can't never did anything.

It is all PERFECT!

Learning is FUN!

Practice makes permanent!

Together we can achieve!

Try? Try not. There is only do or not do. (Yoda)

The greatest people walk through this door.

We can display our positive attitudes both inside and outside the classroom. Refuse to have a bad day. We cannot control what happens to us, but we can control how we respond to the situation — we can control our attitudes! We need to develop activities and situations where positive attitudes are showcased. Teachers and parents can design projects that enable children to capitalize on their individual strengths and foster a positive attitude.

We need to avoid using threats and fear tactics. Fear very quickly shuts down the brain. Remember that motivation is intrinsic; therefore, the use of threats hampers a child's motivation to engage in the learning process. They feel like losers and losers build an "I" against "them" mentality. Please remember that fear is not a good motivator. We want to be friends with our children; not their enemies.

Providing students with feedback is an essential element of the learning process. One type of feedback is non-judgmental — feedback that avoids negative and positive judgments and uses neutral recognition.

Examples of non-judgmental feedback include:

> Let me see if I understand…
>
> Thank you.
>
> I understand what you are doing.
>
> I appreciate your completing the project.
>
> I see that you followed all of the directions correctly.

Experiments have proven that feedback through comments rather than giving numerical scores or grades enhances learning. When grades are given along with written comments on a paper, students tend to ignore the comments and focus on the grade. Teachers that give comments without a grade on the paper report that students engage more productively in improving their work.

Many teachers fear that comments without grades would adversely effect students and elicit negative responses from parents. This fear is not justified. As previously stated, students react positively to the comments and neither parents nor school officials react adversely to these feedback and feedforward statements. In actuality, the use of comments to students helps parents focus on the learning issues rather than on trying to interpret a grade. A numerical score or a grade does not give students advice as to how to improve their work; therefore, an opportunity to enhance learning is lost.

Feedback should include written tasks that encourage students to develop and to understand the key features of what they have learned. Also, comments should identify what the children have done well and should specify what needs improvement. We need to give guidance on how to make the necessary improvements. In short, appropriate feedback should allow thinking to take place. Feedback should enable students the opportunity to utilize assessments as an integral part in the process of learning. (Black, Harrison, Lee, Marshall, & Wiliam, 2004)

Timing is extremely important. There are times that feedback should be given after the child has time to self reflect. The student might need to internalize the situation prior to receiving input from the teacher and/or parent. If a child is feeling down and has a low level of self-efficacy, giving immediate feedback can have detrimental effects. The timing varies on the individual and the particular situation. Usually, frequent feedback is vitally important in the early stages of the learning process. (Rogers, Ludington, & Graham, 1999)

Exposing your child to successful people can enhance one's self-concept. Upon meeting someone who has done it, children begin to believe that they can perform the modeled task. (McAuley, 1985; Schunk, 1985)

I am convinced that learning is a social aspect of human behavior. Social persuasion occurs not in isolation, but in the context of relationships with significant others. (Wigfield, Eccles, & Rodriguez, 1998) Students can remain motivated if they feel secure, safe, and have a sense of belonging. (Hanson, 1998) There is a relationship between a student's sense of belonging and a student's expectations of academic success. (Goodenow, 1991)

Motivating our children is a process. Incorporating "Relevance" and "Responsibility" will assist in this very important endeavor. Remember, our children are our most precious commodity. Let's reward excellence when it is found and continue motivating them as they discover excellence!

Listed below are Doc's helpful hints relating to Motivation and Rewarding Excellence. The hints are suggestions to improve teaching and to assist in the learning process.

DOC'S HELPFUL HINTS:

Be a positive role model.

Students watch a teacher's "every move." Parents and teachers serve as role models for the children. What better way to instill the importance of being positive than to be positive yourself? Being a positive role model is contagious. Please do not accept the philosophy: "do as I say; not as I do."

Show your PASSION for learning and for life.

Love what you do! Let children know that you value life and that you have a love for learning new things. Light the fire! The following mnemonic is an easy way to understand what PASSION is:

Performance: "Find children performing well and reward/celebrate them!

Attitude: Look at the glass as being half-full.

Success: The number one motivator is an opportunity for success!

Support: Give children the required support needed to complete the task.

Individual: Each child MUST feel that he is important—
that he is worthy.

Opportunity: Opportunities need to be relevant, worthwhile, and purposeful.

Novelty: Use a variety of teaching strategies with your children.

Demonstrate that everything is PERFECT!

Each day affords us numerous, new, and exciting opportunities. Instill in your child the attitude that everything is PERFECT! We cannot change what happens to us, but we can control how we respond to it. Teach children to make the best of all situations.

Use appropriate praise.

When appropriate, inform children that their actions are good. A child needs to know that his or her effort and performance are appreciated. Praise increases one's self-efficacy and self-esteem.

Include feedback that is timely, appropriate, and user-friendly.

Make students aware of their progress. In order to make appropriate changes, children need to have feedback that is timely — feedback that is given within one-to-two days after the task was completed. Please make the feedback positive. Instill in the student the behavior that you want; rather than dwelling on the behavior that you do not want.

Use inspirational messages.

Include inspirational quotes, movies, and music in the classroom. They are very motivational and stimulating. These messages are very powerful in creating a positive learning environment.

Stress the importance of effort.

Effort needs to be valued. Children should "feel" that the effort they put forth is appreciated by the teacher and the parent. Effort is an integral part of the learning process.

Encourage your children.

Use praise and feedforward statements daily. Assist with the motivational process by continuously encouraging the children. Let each child know that he or she is valued and that you believe in him or her.

Include positive affirmations.

Keep things positive and upbeat. Affirm the things that students are doing well. Make positive affirmations part of your "classroom talk."

Enjoy the PROCESS of "Discovering Excellence!"

I have included this idea throughout this book. It is a very important concept. Children need to view learning as an enjoyable PROCESS that enables them to "discover excellence." Learning should be FUN!

When one utilizes Doc's helpful hints, students are able to DISCOVER excellence through the use of a PERFECT process!

Chapter 8

Rewarding Excellence!

Self-Esteem

Educating our youth is a very important task in today's society. Today, as never before, educators have tremendous responsibility in molding and educating our young people. It is much easier to educate students when the atmosphere in which the instruction occurs is conducive to learning. Positive self- esteem can be enhanced by utilizing positive reinforcers. A student with a positive self- concept is much easier to educate than one who has cultivated a negative outlook on life.

According to Engle and Snellgrove (1984) motivation is what helps people to behave in one way instead of another. *Motivation* is a hypothetical concept that serves to energize behavior and direct it toward a goal. (Myers, 1990)

Every person is motivated — motivated to have his or her needs met! These *needs*, as presented by Abraham Maslow (1954), are as follows: physiological (food, oxygen, water, sleep, and exercise); safety; belonging and love; esteem; and self-actualization (the confidence in one's ability to be successful in the eyes of others). This is a hierarchy. The needs at the lower level must be met first before the person is ready to move up the chain.

The tremendous opportunity afforded to teachers for the purpose of making a positive impact on the lives of our children should be considered among our society's greatest responsibilities. It can be very challenging for a teacher to meet the needs of each and every child entering the classroom, many of whom are at different levels of development. Creating an environment where each child's needs are able to be met will allow the teacher to effectively motivate the children to learn the objectives of the course. This enriched environment will allow each child to *be someone* and enjoy the learning process.

A great deal of research was completed in the late 1980's and the 1990's pertaining to self-esteem as it relates to motivation and student learning. In this chapter, I will reference some of this valuable research in "setting the stage" for motivating our children today. This valid research will provide great insight for parents and teachers alike.

Nothing affects one's health and energy level quite as much as self-esteem. Young (1993), president and senior consultant of Instruction and Professional Development Inc., states that self-esteem is part of the equation that determines a student's overall school success.

Self-esteem is self regard. It is a composite picture of one's self-value and self-worth. A child must learn self-respect in order to become willing to stand up for his or her self. The value of creating a school environment that promotes positive self-esteem is evident:

The higher a student's self-esteem, the better the student becomes at taking on new challenges.

The higher a student's self-esteem, the better equipped the student will be to cope with diversity.

The higher a student's self-esteem, the more secure he or she will be in confronting obstacles.

The higher a student's self- esteem, the more decisive the student becomes.

The higher a student's self- esteem, the more resilient the student becomes when faced with defeat.

"Believing and achieving" are what schools should be all about. Self-esteem is the educator's legacy to the students. In today's world, with the challenges of our modern workforce, it is extremely important to help children achieve a level of self-esteem that can produce an inner strength and assist in the motivational process. Also, we need to encourage our students to develop a desire to achieve and excel and to care for themselves as well as others. (Young, 1993)

Friedland (1992) said that researchers have demonstrated a correlation between good learning outcomes and high self-esteem. Dozens of reputable research studies show a high correlation between healthy self-esteem and the following behaviors: superior academic achievement; less chance of dropping out of school; and higher educational aspirations.

Healthy self-esteem is an important factor in the development of a successful attitude in any young person. (Friedland, 1992)

Our level of *achievement motivation* is often dependent on our personal outlook. There are certain situations that may optimize motivation for specific individuals while others may respond to them differently. Motivation is something people can share but it is also highly dependent on an individual's ability to respond positively in a given situation. In order to effectively motivate others, we must find the best matches between our motivational techniques and the people and situations involved.

One must find the correct stimuli to motivate each individual. (Maehr, 1974) Parents and teachers must look at each person as an individual and create for that person an environment that will be conducive to motivation. People must feel free to take risks. The stimuli should be present to create a risk-free environment for each individual involved. Students must know and believe that it is okay to make mistakes. Learning is a work in progress.

Learning should never be strictly an academic exercise, instead it should be something personal and meaningful to the students involved. Students will invest effort in an activity and/or project if they believe that they can accomplish something worthwhile.

Learning exercises can be very competitive which creates a win/lose mentality. Children who have not had much success in school will see very little point in continuing to try. In handling this situation, the type of feedback given is extremely important. In a competitive system, low achievers attribute their performance to lack of ability. High achievers will give credit to their effort. In a process oriented system, all students begin to attribute performance to effort. As a result, academic achievement is improved – especially among low achievers. (Black, Harrison, Lee, Marshall, & Wiliam, 2004)

Motivation can be broken down into two categories: *intrinsic motivation* and *extrinsic motivation.* Intrinsic motivation comes from within a person rather than an outside source. Extrinsic motivation, on the other hand, is inspired by an external stimulus that assists in changing a behavior.

Incentives are extrinsic motivators that are used to motivate a student. An incentive can include recognition, special privileges, and tangible awards. It is quite evident according to Shanker *(1990)* that schools must reform their incentive programs and provide additional incentives. Incentives are very much needed to assist with the education of our young people. Systems that have ignored financial incentives have not been successful. Some students are bored and need incentives to motivate them to remain in school. (Shanker, 1990)

According to B. F. Skinner (Holland, 1992), when people learn to describe contingencies and to act on descriptives of contingencies they begin to have a different basis for responding than the direct shaping of behavior by reinforcement. Reinforcing appropriate behavior pays big dividends. *Reinforcers* include incentives that reward student achievement.

Change is important. By using Skinner's fundamental discovery of frequency or response rate (the rate of change) we are beginning to discover important relations among problem solving and retention. (Johnson & Layng, 1992) In the review by Sizer (1983) on the National Report, one finds that importance should be given on providing incentives for students.

External events appear to "strengthen" the behavior which has preceded the occurrence of the external event. Several comparative studies have shown that the amount of reinforcement is an effective variable in certain situations. (Miller & Estes, 1961) Incentives lead to arousal; therefore, causing reinforcement to change behaviors. (Cofer, 1972) Incentives can lead to positive self-esteem which ultimately improves one's entire self-concept. The development of a positive *self-concept* is necessary for an individual to become an effective learner. (Healey, 1969) Our self-concept comes to regulate our many behaviors. As positive reinforcements are increased, the self-concept grows in esteem. Self-concept has an affective component, called self-esteem, and it has a function which allows one to predict and guide behavior. (Dusek, 1987) In general, measures of self-concept are positively correlated with grades earned in school. Children with high self-esteem receive higher grades than children with low self-esteem. (Dusek, 1987)

Most students, particularly "at-risk" students, need motivation in order to improve academic performance. Incentive plans can assist in improving the *esprit-de-corps* of the school community. Motivation can enhance academic success as well as improve a student's chances for success in society. (Wircenski & Sarkees, 1990)

I have encountered several schools which use incentive plans very effectively. Some of the program goals that these schools use include:

Improving school attendance.

Decreasing the dropout rate.

Improving student academic performance.

Decreasing the number of discipline problems.

In 1994, I conducted a research study to determine whether or not incentive programs made a difference in senior high schools across the state of Indiana. The study attempted to determine whether or not incentive programs affect student grades and attendance issues.

The study put emphasis on the relationship between selected student incentives and the average daily attendance rates, student dropout rates, and academic performance in Indiana senior high schools. Five questions provided the focus for the research. Question one focused on whether or not the schools utilized a student incentive program. Question two through five focused on the incentive categories as they pertained to attendance and academic achievement. The intent of the study was to determine whether or not special recognition, special privileges, and/or tangible awards had an effect on the average daily attendance rates, dropout rates, and increases in grade point averages. The following conclusions were derived from the study:

1. Recognition, special privileges, and tangible awards have a positive effect on average daily attendance rates.

2. Recognition, special privileges, and tangible awards have a positive effect on dropout rates.

3. Recognition, special privileges, and tangible awards have a positive effect on students generally earning all A's and B's.

4. Recognition, special privileges, and tangible awards
have a positive effect on students generally earning
C's and D's as opposed to receiving failing grades.

Even though this study dealt with high school students,
my experiences make me believe that the conclusions
are relevant to children of all ages.

Achieving success assists in improving one's self-
esteem. Hopefully, the information I have presented
in this chapter will help you in developing and
maintaining high levels of self-esteem in your children.

*Listed below are Doc's helpful hints relating to Rewarding
Excellence. The hints are suggestions to improve teaching
and to assist in the learning process.*

DOC'S HELPFUL HINTS:

Include student incentives in the learning process.

Include recognition, special privileges, and tangible
awards as part of the incentive plan.

Include students in determining the rewards to use.

Communication between parents and teachers should
take place regularly to assure that the same process is
being used both at home and at school.

Let the children know you VALUE them!! Catch students
doing good things and reward them for the behavior!!

As one can determine after reading the chapter, self-
esteem is very important in the educational process of
each individual person. Both parents and teachers benefit from the utilization of incentives as an extrinsic motivator. The ultimate goal is for each person to become

intrinsically motivated to learn.

I contend that the extrinsic reward system will assist in the process of developing intrinsic motivation. We need a combination of both intrinsic and extrinsic rewards. Children need to experience both intrinsic and extrinsic rewards in order to fully develop their talents.
(Csikszentmihalyi et al., 1993)

As the old saying goes, "You can lead a horse to water, but you can't make him drink." I contend that extrinsic motivation is the salt needed to make people thirsty! The following mnemonic device will assist in the development of high self-esteem.

Students
Expect
Love and support
From

Everyone
Surrounding
Them;
Especially
Early in the
Maturation process!

When one utilizes Doc's helpful hints, students are able to DISCOVER excellence through the use of a PERFECT process!

Chapter 9

Motivational Strategies

Motivational Strategies

There are numerous theories on motivation. Psychologists are continually trying to find the right answer when it comes to motivating people. Parents and teachers are constantly in search of ways to motivate their children. I have a secret for you.... *"Everyone is motivated!"* Yes, every single human being. We are motivated to have our *needs* met! I mentioned this in the previous chapter but feel that it needs to be stated again.

According to Hal Urban, we need to search for a reason why *we can* instead of a reason why *we cannot.* The limitations we have are self-imposed. If we truly believe that we cannot succeed, then we won't—not until we exchange our negative beliefs for a new set of positive beliefs. There are a number of resources written on this subject which claim that we can reach a higher level of potential and increase our feeling of self-worth if we will only allow ourselves to be more positive. This, in turn, will give us the confidence to attempt new things — even risking failure. (Urban, 2003)

Teachers have the opportunity to challenge each child to tap into the positive. By creating a risk-free learning environment that meets the needs of all children, teachers can encourage students to take the necessary risks to learn that they can succeed. *You can do it!*

Creative problem solving skills are facilitated by teachers who promote positive feelings. (Isen, 1999, 2001) Students are happy when their attention is focused upon attaining the desired consequences of their actions, whereas fear develops when attention is focused upon the potential of failure and humiliation. (Stein & Levine, 1987) In other words, students need to know that there will be a significant positive payoff for their hard work and efforts if they succeed and that the negative consequences of failure will be minimal. The focus should be on the process; not necessarily on whether or not the student completes the task "correctly."

Anxiety and fear tend to interfere with the learning process. (Brosnan, 1998; Stipek, 2002) High levels of anxiety decrease academic performance. On the other hand, students low in anxiety tend to be better risk-takers. (Tohill & Holyoak, 2000)

Students will more freely attempt tasks if they believe they are competent and believe they have a degree of control over the outcome. (Bandura, 1997; Brophy, 1998) Students who believe they are capable of accomplishing a task are usually more persistent. They will increase their efforts even in the face of failure, whereas students who believe they cannot succeed give up more easily or avoid the task altogether. (Bandura, 1997; Burger, 1992; Schunk, 1985; Schwartzer, 1992)

Resnick (1999) contends that effort actually creates ability — that people can become smarter by working harder. Hard work truly does pay off. There is a positive relationship between a student's sense of belonging and his or her expectations of academic success. (Goodenow, 1991)

In short, students need to have an environment where their basic needs are being met, they feel good about themselves, they trust the facilitator, and they enjoy the learning process. They should feel that the learning environment exists to benefit them in every way possible.

The remainder of this chapter includes twenty things that I have found to assist teachers in their endeavors to create such an environment. These ideas have greatly assisted me in developing and/or increasing the child's inner drive to yearn for success. They are simple concepts; *but effective!*

Listed below are Doc's helpful hints relating to Motivational Strategies. The hints are suggestions to improve teaching and to assist in the learning process.

DOC'S HELPFUL HINTS:

Motivational handraising.

All students must raise their hand whenever the teacher asks a question. If a student knows the answer to the question, the student will display four fingers. If a student thinks he or she knows the answer, but is not sure, the student will display three fingers. If the student does not understand the question, the student will display two fingers. If the student does not know the answer, the student will display only one finger. This way, no one is ostracized for not knowing the correct answer.

I recommend that the teacher call on the student who normally does not raise a hand in class when that student has displayed four fingers. After answering a question correctly in front of peers, the student's self-esteem will truly soar to new heights!

"I – Pass"

Give your students the option to say "I pass" when called upon by the teacher if they do not know the answer. This keeps students from being "put-on-the-spot" and feeling embarrassed if they cannot think of the answer. Fear of embarrassment is diminished; therefore, the brain is more able to concentrate and remain engaged in the thinking process.

Open-palm.

When addressing students, identifying them, and/or taking attendence, teachers should use an open-palm instead of pointing their index finger. (Turn your hand with the palm facing upward and point your hand toward the student.) The open palm is "an invitation"' rather than a negative symbol like the pointing finger which might begin to plant negative thoughts and feelings in the child's brain. The pointed finger, in our culture, is seen as a negative gesture; therefore, does not create on open, positive learning environment.

Paper distribution.

Whenever handing papers to students, the teacher should personally hand each student his or her copy and make eye-contact with each student. This assists in creating a risk-free, brain-compatible, caring classroom environment. You are "telling" each student that he or she is important to you!

Missing-In-Action (MIA) time.

If a student comes to class on time, prepared to learn, and actively participates in class throughout the week, that student will receive ten to fifteen minutes of "free" time on the last class period of the week. The student can use this time to complete educational activities of his or her choice (homework assignments, reading, etc.).

If a child chooses not to complete the assigned work, chooses not to come to class on time, chooses not to be prepared for class, chooses to misbehave in class, etc., this student will be considered "missing-in-action"; there-fore, the student should use that ten to fifteen minutes at the end of the week to compensate for the loss of educa-tion due to his or her poor choices. This student would complete the original (traditional) assignments that were not turned in on time while others are enjoying their "free" time.

Study time (prior to going to sleep).

Robert Stickgold, of Harvard Medical School, reports that sleep is what assists learning and memory. Volunteers were trained in a task of visual learning and then tested to establish their baseline performance. When periodically retested during the day, no improvement over the baseline was made. After a good night of sleep, they performed significantly better. It takes sleep to convert temporary memories into long-term learning. (Ackerman, 2004) Recommend that your students study prior to going to bed instead of "cramming" the morning of a test.

Laughter.

It is reported by Dr. William Fry of Stanford University that the body reacts biochemically to laughing. Fry inserted catheters into the veins of medical student who were watching and listening to a comedian. He and his associate Lee Berk of the Loma Linda Medical School found a change in the chemical balance of the blood which is believed to boost the body's production of the neurotransmitters needed for alertness and memory. (Jenson, 1995) I recommend that it should be a "norm" for students to laugh at school and at home. Learning should be FUN. Allow or even provoke a good laugh whenever possible!!

Exercise to increase "smartness."

University of Illinois researchers point out that aerobic exercise, including brisk walking, not only strengthens our muscles and improves our cardiovascular system, it also assists the brain in the learning process. Exercise helps bulk up the brain. (Kotulak, 2004) I recommend that you encourage your children get plenty of exercise. Encourage children to physically play instead of just playing games that require them to sit in one spot for extended periods of time without much moving about. Instead of watching hours of television, encourage your children to play an active game or exercise in order to assist them with both physical and mental fitness.

Down-time.

The brain needs down-time. Down-time or *processing-time* is something that most students already use effectively, whether or not the teacher appropriates it. They will tune out what is going on around them, including the teacher. Down-time enables the new synapses that were formed during the learning process to be strengthened. They can be strengthened only when no other neurostimuli are competing with them. This processing time has to be a non-challenging time.

Turn off the television.

Frequent television watching by infants and toddlers may shorten their attention span by the age of seven. Our brains rapidly change early in life. Animal research shows that the type of stimulation we receive can "rewire" the brain. Things happen quickly on television; therefore, children's brains may come to expect this pace, making it more difficult to concentrate if there's less stimulation, says study leader Dimitri Christakis. Also, the television time replaces other activities such as reading and play which are essentials in helping with the learning and motivational process. (Elias, 2004)

Greet students "at the door."

A teacher should meet each student at the classroom door with a smile and refer to each student by his or her first name. This personalization strikes the emotions and assists in making the classroom an enriched environment where everyone is *someone.* Hearing our first name makes us feel important. This also gives the teacher time to say something positive to each child as he or she enters the room.

Use applause.

Seek opportunities to use applause in the classroom. Being recognized by our peers is an ego booster. One's self-esteem is increased when applause is given. It is one of society's ways of saying, "You are okay!" You might even give students a standing ovation!

Use celebrations.

Our attention span is no longer than fifteen to twenty minutes. In fact, many of us have attention spans of only seven to ten minutes. We need to have "state-changes" (the opportunity to change positions by getting out of our chairs and energizing ourselves) every twenty to thirty minutes. An ideal way of handling this task is to lead a celebration. This is an act that requires the students to complete something physical and upbeat such as reaching for the stars or performing the "wave." These fun activities last approximately one minute or less and tell the brain that something good just happened — learning a concept just occurred! Why not celebrate learning?!!

Send positive notes home.

Children love to receive mail and they love to hear

good things about themselves. Catch students doing good things and write a note to their parents and tell them what they did that was exemplary. This reinforces the behaviors that we want in the classroom and at home while at the same time improving the student's self-esteem. You are making a very important connection with the student and his or her parents.

Give "mistake coupons."

Prepare coupons for each student that read, "I made a mistake and I am learning!" This sends the message that we want our children to be educated risk-takers. Students need to know that it is alright to stretch themselves and to try new things even if mistakes are made. Have students give you a coupon whenever they recognize that they made a mistake. Accept the coupon, pat the student on the back, give the student another coupon, and encourage the student to continue taking risks and having FUN in the learning process.

Use appropriate eye movement.

The movement of our eyes provide clues as to our thinking styles. In performing certain tasks, we tend to move our eyes to certain areas of our face; therefore, focusing on specific areas of the room. (Rogers, Ludington, & Graham, 1999) Five quick tips for improving student learning:

> Stand to the right side of the classroom (from the students' perspective) when presenting new ideas.

> Stand to the left side of the room when reviewing information.

Place student assignments on the wall..

1. Above eye level for easier recall of information.
2. At eye level if you are going to discuss the information.
3. Below eye level to foster "feelings" about the information.

"WOW!" Them.

Excite students about learning. Learning should be fun and enjoyable. Begin the class with an activity and/or situation that intrigues the students and causes them to want to know more. Assist students in finding the connectedness and the importance of learning the objective(s) of the lesson. The **"WOW"** affect capitalizes on student emotions which influence motivation, recall, decision-making, problem-solving, and learning.

Create an enriched environment.

Make the classroom inviting — make it look like home. Decorate the walls with positive, warm sayings and pictures. Have rugs on the floor, plants in the room, and music playing in the background. You could even mount a refrigerator door on a wall to place student accomplishments on, just like home! An enriched environment is needed to assist in the learning process.

Use music.

From a very early age, neural pathways are being formed. Immersion in musical experiences establishes more neural pathways throughout the brain, which ultimately allows the brain to function better. Music can be used to assist with reading readiness, language acquisition, and cognitive development.

I recommend that music be used in the classroom — it is a powerful learning instrument. Music helps "create an enriched learning environment." Play music to introduce a lesson, to segue into a new area of the lesson, and/or to conclude the learning segment.

One's self-esteem can also be fostered through the use of music. Music instruction actually enhances student achievement in areas outside of music.

Be yourself.

Let students know you are "human." Share things about yourself with the students. Have pictures of important people in your life on your desk. Demonstrate the passion you have for teaching and learning. Let students know you are believable and trustworthy. They need to know you are teaching because you care!

When one utilizes Doc's helpful hints, students are able to DISCOVER excellence through the use of a PERFECT process!

Conclusion

I had the opportunity of leading a workshop for parents in the town in which I had previously been the high school principal. As parents were entering the room, I recognized one particular parent that had not been very pleased with me during my years as an administrator. Her son had been in numerous situations in which he did not make appropriate choices; therefore, I had to end up recommending expulsion for the young man. This particular mother would not speak to me after this situation had occured.

The title of the program I was presenting that evening was "Your Child and Mine," and I started the evening by describing the song, "One Voice." I explained the significance that we, as individuals, can have on our young people and the fact that each of us can be the "one voice" that saves the life of a child and enables him or her to feel good about what he or she does in life.

After the workshop, the mother waited around to talk to me. I was getting nervous, in anticipation of what she might have to say. Then I noticed that she had tears streaming down her face. She walked over to me and whispered in my ear, "Thank you — you were that 'one voice' to my son. You never gave up on him. Even though you had to recommend him for expulsion, you continued to call and talk with him and truly made him believe in himself."

WOW! These were the best words that I could have heard. The mother went on to share how successful he was as an adult. He was graduating from college and looking forward to a successful future.

Our children are our most precious commodity! As I mentioned in my introduction, I want other teachers and parents to experience the joys of helping others in life so that they can discover excellence. My journey as an educator and father has been rewarding and FUN!! We need to remember to treat our students as we would want others to treat our own children!!

I have been blessed with a wonderful family. My role as a father has been very important to me. I have tried to use the real "3 R's" at home and to model them for my children. My oldest son, Jared, is currently a fourth class cadet at the United States Air Force Academy. On my 44th birthday, just after Jared had successfully completed the Basic Cadet Training (or what the cadets refer to as "Beast") and prior to attending his first academic class at the Academy, he sent me a letter containing the following:

"Listen, my sons, to a father's discipline, and pay attention so that you may gain understanding, for I am giving you good instruction. Don't abandon my teaching. When I was a son my father, tender and precious to my mother, he taught me and said: Your heart must hold on to my words. Keep my commands and live. Get wisdom, get understanding; don't forget or turn away from the words of my mouth."

Proverbs 4: vs. 1-5

"Dad, I was reading in my military Bible tonight in Proverbs and I saw this set of verses. I couldn't think of a better way to put what you have brought to "my table." Your example to me of hard work and dedication makes this place seem easier. School starts in five days, and I'm a little nervous about that, but I know with hard work and dedication, I can make it out here. I know you won't get this letter for a couple of days after your birthday, but I saw those verses and I thought of you. So, that's my other birthday present for you."

- Jared Freeman

He was correct, a father could not ask for any better birthday present than that. Knowing that your son has gained from the life that you have lived, the love that you have given, and the instruction that you have modeled, is the most rewarding accomplishment you can earn!!

Hopefully, this book has given you some information to assist you in getting back to the basics — the true "Three R's" which are: **Relevance, Responsibility, and Rewarding Excellence.**

We never know when we will be that "one voice" that a child needs to hear, that one voice that makes the difference in the child's life.

Good luck!!

Sources Cited

Ackerman, S. (2004). "The Remarkably Busy Sleeping Brain." Brain Work 14(1): 3-4.

Armstrong, T. (1994). Multiple Intelligences in the Classroom. Alexandria, VA: ASCD.

Bandura, A. (1997). Self-efficacy: The Exercise of Control. New York: W.H. Freeman.

Berliner, D. C., & Biddle, B. J. (1995). Manufactured Crisis: Myths, Fraud, and the Attack on America's Public Schools. Reading, MA: Addison-Wesley.

Binet, A., & Simon, T. (1905). "Methods Nouvelles Pour le Diagnoatique du Niveau Intellectu 2el Desanormaux [New Methods for the Diagnosis of the Intellectual Level of the Abnormal]". L'annee Psychologique, 11, 236-245.

Black, P., Harrison, C., Lee, C., Marshall, B., & Wiliam, D. (2004). "Working Inside the Black Box: Assessment for Learning in the Classroom." Phi Delta Kappan, 86 (1): 9-21.

Boggiano, A. K., & Katz, P. (1991). "Maladaptive Achievement Patterns in Students: The Role of Teachers' Controlling Strategies." Journal of Social Issues, 47(4), 35-51.

Brophy, J. (1996). Classroom Management as Socializing Students Into Clearly Articulated Roles. Paper presented at the annual meeting of the American Educational Research Association, New York.

Brophy, J. E. (1998) Motivating Students to Learn. Boston: McGraw-Hill.

Brosnan, M. J. (1998). "The Impact of Computer Anxiety and Self-Efficacy Upon Performance." Journal of Computer_Assisted Learning, 14(3), 223-234.

Burger, J. M. (1992). Desire for Control: Personality, Social and Clinical Perspectives. New York: Plenum Press.

Butler, R., & Nisan, M. (1986). "Effects of no Feedback, Task-related Comments, and Grades on Intrinsic Motivation and Performance" Journal of Educational Psychology, 78, 210-216.

Cameron, J. & Pierce, W. D. (2002). Rewards and Intrinsic Motivation: Resolving the Controversy. Westport, CT: Bergin & Garvey.

Cofer, C. N. (1972). Motivation & Emotion. Illinois: Scott, Foresman, and Company.

Csikszentmihalyi, M. (1985). "The Flow Experience and its Significance for Human Psychology." In M. Csikszentmihalyi & I. S. Csikszentmihalyi (Eds.), Optimal Experience: Psychological Studies of Flow in Consciousness (pp. 15-36). New York: Cambridge University Press.

Csikszentmihalyi, M., Rathunde, K., & Whalen, M. (1993). Talented Teenagers: The Roots of Success and Failure. New York: Cambridge University Press.

D'Arcangelo, M., Diamond, M., Wolfe, P., Sylwester, R., Caine, G., & Caine, R. (2004). The Brains Behind the Brain: Five Prominent Educators and Researchers Discuss How the Brain Learns.

Retrieved August 2004 from: http://www.owl.org.

Dusek, J. B. (1987). Adolescent Development and Behavior. Englewood Cliffs, New Jersey: Prentice-Hall.

Elias, M. (2004, April). "TV Stimulation May Be 'Rewiring Children's Brains.'" USA Today. April 5, 2004, Pg. D5.

Engle, T. L., & Snellgrove, L. (1984). Psychology: Its Principles and Applications, (8th ed). Florida: Harcourt Brace Johanovich.

Fogarty, R. (1997). Brain Compatible Classrooms. Arlington Heights: SkyLight Professional Development.

Friedland, S. (1992, January). "Building Student Self-Esteem for School Improvement". National Association of Secondary School Principals Bulletin. Pp. 96-106.

Friedman, M. I., & Lackey, G. H. (1991) The Psychology of Human Control: A General Theory of Purposeful Behavior. New York: Praeger.

Gardner, H. (1983). Frames of Mind: The Theory of Multiple Intelligences. New York: BasicBooks.

Gardner, H. (1993). Multiple Intelligences: The Theory in Practice. New York, NY: BasicBooks.

Gardner, H. (1995, November). "Reflections on Multiple Intelligences: Myths and Messages." Phi Delta Kappan, 77(3), 200-209.

Goodenow, C. (1991). The Sense of Belonging and its Relationship to Academic Motivation Among Pre- and Early Adolescent Students. Paper presented at the annual meeting of the American Educational Research Association, Chicago.

Haggerty, B. A. (1995). Nurturing Intelligences: A Guide to Multiple Intelligences Theory and Teaching. Menlo Park, CA: Addison-Wesley.

Hanson, K. K. (1998). "Get Students Going: Motivation in the Middle Grades." Schools in the Middle, 8(1), 28-33.

Harth, J. (1995). The Creative Loop. Reading, Mass,: Addison-Wesley.

Healy, J. (1990). Endangered Minds. New York: Touchstone.

Henley, G. W. (1969). Self-Concept: A Comparison of Negro, Anglo, and Spanish American Students Across Ethnic, Sex, and Socioeconomic Variables. California: R and E. Research Associates.

Holland, J. (1992, May). " B. F. Skinner (1904-1990)." American Psychology, 47, 665-667.

Isen, A. M. (1999). "Positive Affect. In T. Dalgleilsh & M. J. Power (Eds.), Handbook of cognition and emotion (pp. 521-539). Chichester, England: John Wiley & Sons.

Jacobs, W. J., and Nadel, L. (1985) "Stress—Induced Recovery of Fears and Phobias." Psychological Review 92, 4: 512-531.

Jensen, E. (1995). The Learning Brain. San Diego: The Brain Store, Inc.

Jensen, E. (1998). Teaching With The Brain In Mind. Alexandria: Association for Supervision and Curriculum Development.

Jensen, E. (1998). Introduction to Brain-Compatible Learning. San Diego: The Brain Store, Inc.

Johnson, K. & Layng, T. V. (1992). "Breaking the Structuralist Barrier." American Psychologist, 47, 1475-1490.

Jones, K . (2004). "A Balanced School Accountability Model: An Alternative to High-Stakes Testing." Phi Delta Kappan 85 (8): 584-590.

Kornhaber, M., Krechevsky, M., & Gardner, H. (1990). "Engaging Intelligence." Educational Psychologist, 25(3-4), 177-199.

Kotulak, R. (2004, March). "Exercise for the Body is Food for Brain, Study Says." Chicago Tribune. March 17, 2004: p. C1.

Krechevsky, M., & Gardner, H. (1990). "Multiple Intelligences, Multiple Chances." In D. E. Inbar (Ed.), Second Chance in Education: An Interdisciplinary and International Perspective (pp. 69-88). New York: Falmer Press.

Lazear, D. G. (1991). Seven Ways of Teaching: The Artistry of Teaching With Multiple Intelligences. Palatine, IL: SkyLight.

Lundin, S., Paul, H. & Christensen, J. (1995). Fish. New York: Hyperion.

Lunenburg, F. C., & Schmidt, L. J. (1989). "Pupil Control Ideology, Pupil Control Behavior and the Quality of School Life." Journal of Research and Development in Education, 22, 36-44.

Maehr. M. L. (1974). Sociocultural Origins of Achievement. California: Wadsworth Publishing Company, Inc.

Maslow, A. H. (1954). Motivation and Personality. New York: Harper & Row.

McAuley, E. (1985). "Modeling and Self-Efficacy: A test of Bandura's Model." Journal of Sport Psychology, 7, 283-295.

Miller, L., & Estes, B. (1961). "Monetary Reward and Motivation in Discrimination Learning." Journal of Experimental Psychology, 61, 501-504.

Mitchell, T. G. (1985). "Sociological Implications of the Flow Experience." In M. Csikszentmihalyi & I. S. Csikszemtmihalyi (Eds.), Optimal Experience: Psychological Studies of Flow in Consciousness (pp. 36-59). New York: Cambridge University Press.

Moorman, C. (2001). Spirit Whisperers. Merrill, Michigan: Personal Power Press.

Mueller, C. M., & Dweck, C. S. (1998). "Praise for Intelligence Can Undermine Children's Motivation and Performance." Journal of Personality & Social Psychology, 75(1), 33-52.

Myers, D. (1990). Exploring Psychology. New York: Worth Publishers, Inc.

Nowicki, S., & Barnes, J. (1973). "Effects of a Structured Camp Experience on Locus of Control Orientation of Inner-City Children." Journal of Genetic Psychology, 122, 247-262.

Page, E. B. (1958). "Teacher Comments and Student Performance: A Seventy-four Classroom Experiment in School Motivation." Journal of Educational Psychology, 49, 173-181.

Pierce, J. & Newstrom, J. (1993). The Manager's Bookshelf: A Mosaic of Contemporary Views. 3rd ed. New York: HarperCollins College Publishers, Inc.

Resinck, L . B. (1999). "From Aptitude to Effort: A New Foundation for our Schools." American Educator, 23(1), 14-17.

Rogers, S., Ludington, J., & Graham, S. (1999). Motivation & Learning. Evergreen, Colorado: Peak Learning Systems, Inc.

Ryan, R. M., & Deci, E. L . (2000). "When Rewards Compete With Nature: The Undermining of Intrinsic Motivation and Self-regulation." In C. Sansone & J. M. Harackiewicz (Eds.), Intrinsic and extrinsic motivation: The search for optimal motivation and performance (pp. 14-54). San Diego, CA: Academic Press.

Schunk, D. H. (1985). "Self-efficacy and Classroom Learning." Psychology in the School, 22, 208-223.

Schunk, D. H., & Zimmerman, B. J. (1996). "Modeling and Self-efficacy Influences on Children's Development of Self-Regulation." In J. Juvonen & K. R. Wentzel (Eds.), Social Motivation: Understanding Children's School Adjustment (pp. 154-180). New York: Cambridge University Press.

Schwartzer, R. (Ed.,). (1992). Self-Efficacy: Thought Control of Action. Washington, DC: Hemisphere.

Sedek, G., & McIntosh, D. N. (1998). "Intellectual Helplessness: Domain Specificity, Teaching Styles, and School Achievement." In M. Kofta, G. Weary, & G. Sedek (Eds.), Personal Control in Action: Cognitive and Motivational Mechanisms (pp. 419-443). New York: Plenum.

Shanker, A. (1990). "The End of the Traditional Model of Schooling and a Proposal for Using Incentives to Restructure One Public School." Phi Delta Kappan, 71, 345-357.

Sizer, T. (1983). "A Review and Comment on the National Report." National Association of Secondary School Principal. VA: Reston.

Stein, N. L., & Levine, L. J. (1987). "Thinking About Feelings: The Development and Organization of Emotional Knowledge." In R. E. Snow & M. J. Farr (Eds.), Aptitude, Learning, and Instruction (Vol. 3) (pp. 165-197). Hillsdale, NJ: Erlbaum.

Stipek, D. J. (2002). Motivation to Learn: From Theory to Practice (4th ed.). Boston: Allyn and Bacon.

Tang, T. L., & Sarsfield-Baldwin, L. (1991). "The Effects of Self-Esteem, Task Label, and Performance Feedback on Task Liking and Intrinsic Motivation." The Journal of Social Psychology, 131(4), 567-572.

The New Lexicon Webster's Dictionary of the English Language. (1989). New York: Lexicon Publications, Inc.

Tohill, J. M. & Holyoak, K. J. (2000). "The Impact of Anxiety on Analogical Reasoning." Thinking & Reasoning, 6(1), 27-40.

Urban, H. (2003). Life's Greatest Lessons: 20 Things That Matter. 4th ed. New York: Simon & Schuster.

Wircenski, J., & Sarkees, N. (1990, April). "Instructional Alternatives: Rescue Strategies for At-risk Students." National Association of Secondary School Principals Curriculum Report, 19, 1-5.

Youngs, B. B. (1993, January). "Self-Esteem in the School: More than a "Feel-Good" Movement." National Association of Secondary School Principal Bulletin, 59-66.

Zahorik, J. A. (1994). Making Things Interesting. Paper presented at the annual meeting of the American Educational Research Association, New Orleans, LA.